A Nortł

A L MOTTLEY

Disclaimer: This is a work of non-fiction containing references to real locations and situations based on the recall of the author. If, on reading this, you feel that there are any inaccuracies in any of the salient details, please bring it to the attention of the publishers immediately.

Published by Any Subject Books

Website: http:/www.anysubject.com

Facebook: http:/www.facebook.com/anysubject

Cover image: http://www.canstockphoto.com

ISBN: 978-1-909392-53-3

DEDICATION

To all my family and friends for their support and endurance.

Thank you everyone for making this book a possibility.

For the best Mam ever.

CONTENTS

AN ODE TO MANCHESTER

If you can chat with everyone in the shop - and not lose your place in the queue,

Or walk with snobs whilst wearing a pinny - and not feel mithered, much,

If neither the rent man nor bailiff can find you

And you can count on the neighbours for a 'touch',

If you can fill the wait at the bus stop

With tales of struggle and bad luck,

Yours is the North and everything in it

And - which is more - you're a Manc, chuck.

With apologies to Rudyard Kipling

ACKNOWLEDGMENTS

I could fill another book with 'Thank you's' so I'll do my best to keep it short. If you don't see your name here, don't think you've been forgotten. I'll get round to you in the next book!

Firstly immense thanks to Clive and Damaris at Any Subject Books, without whom there wouldn't be a book. Your kindness and faith in me has been heart warming. Your professional advice, invaluable. I never knew how much work went into getting scribbled musings into 'print' and I will be forever grateful to you all for taking a chance on me.

To all my 'social media' friends who enjoyed my little stories and encouraged me to go the whole hog and write an actual book. Too many to mention, but I'd like to single out (and show up) Vic Carey, who was the first person to say: "You should write a book."

Thank you also to the many people who 'jogged' my memory and contributed to the Mancunian Dictionary, in particular: Maggie Machin, Marie Zakarraya, Tracey Green, Linda Pohl, Thomas Dale, Sue Macmillan, Elizabeth Whittaker, Sherril Wright, Margaret Maylett, Christine Holt, Anita Mckimm, Angela Stewart, Carmel Flanagan, Jo Dolan Derrig, Ann Roddy and Betty Halfpenny.

To my wonderful friends Rayella, Julie and Jean who allowed me to neglect them and listened to me waffling on about book this and book that.

To my beloved football team Manchester City, not that they did anything in regard of this book but I'll mention them any chance I can get.

Finally my wonderful family. Every single one of them. Without them I wouldn't even have a book to acknowledge. I love you all to bits even if I did try to kill some of you in the past. Dad, I wish you had been here to see this, but I believe in heaven and know you are up there looking down on me proudly. Mam, you're an absolute nutter and I wouldn't have it any other way. You are comedy gold but aside from that you gave me, my sisters and 'r Wayne (the Chosen One) the best upbringing a child could have. You kept us safe, fed and watered but above all else you gave us unconditional love and taught us the value of loyalty.

To my children Nadine, Kez and Tahrah I love you and I hope I have been an embarrassing mum to you on at least one occasion. Thank you for your forgiveness when I have been less than perfect and thank you for my beautiful grandchildren (Jon-Paul, wherever you are, I hope you are happy).

One final thank you and that goes to the city of Manchester. Best city in the world. I will be eternally grateful that fate graced me with such a wonderful hometown

PROLOGUE

Joyce Holden watched sulkily as the woman in the next bed carefully dressed her baby. She had watched women come and go. Come in fat and alone. Go out a little less fat and accompanied by a baby, or sometimes two.

She walked wearily to the nursery.

"You can tell this place used to be a bleeding workhouse," she mumbled to herself.

Bare brick walls, painted in a pale mustard, with accents of the same sickly green that covered the walls of her bedroom at Mam and Dad's house. She'd covered it, as much as possible, with pictures of Frankie Vaughn and Victor Mature. She most definitely had a 'type,' tall and dark. She smiled to herself, and then a pang of sadness washed over her. He would have been here if he could ...

She continued down the dreary corridor. Two midwives passed. She looked back and saw that they were looking back, too. She gave the icy stare that she would become expert at in years to come. They returned looks of contempt and carried on up the corridor.

She arrived at the wall of glass at the front of the nursery and peered through, as if looking through a shop window, selling what? Cots? Babies? She giggled to herself. It would be good if she could buy one, especially after what she'd just been through during labour. Never again! Famous last words. "Bottle time again, Mrs Holden?" said the midwife, who upon seeing Joyce's nose pressed up against the glass had opened the door, baby in one hand ,bottle in the other, standing there short, fat and pink-faced, not unlike a baby herself. Short woman, giant baby.

Joyce had noticed the emphasis on 'Mrs' and the tone. She twisted the wedding ring Mam had made her wear. *She can kiss my arse. She knows damn well I'm not married. The COW.*

"Where's my daughter?" The midwife gave a snooty sniff before pointing. "Over there, in the corner."

Joyce walked over to the cot and her heart exploded. There, swaddled and bound in a pink blanket lay the most beautiful human being she had ever seen. Chocolate brown hair and a tiny face peeped out from under the blanket. She looked just like one of the girls in *Mutiny on the Bounty*. "Come here, sweetheart," she cooed, picking up the baby ever so gently. The baby scrunched her nose and appeared to be peeping at her. "Are you looking at Mummy? Mummy's going to feed you, change you and decide on a name for you. What about Kimberly? I like Kimberly."

1

She carried on, talking softly, saying words that made no sense to the possible Kimberly. Possible Kimberly sucked on her bottle, and looked up at this big, soft and noisy person.

"Awww. She's studying me ... I'm your Mummy, little lady ... I wonder what's going on in that tiny little head of yours?"

Possible Kimberly stopped sucking, for a second as if to say 'Do you mind? And less of the tiny. You've given birth to a genius here. Anyway stop prattling on, I'm eating. Don't know about you, but I've had a traumatic few weeks and I'd like me tea in peace.' Mummy spotted a copy of *Woman's Realm* and settled down to read, while baby carried on developing a taste for Ostermilk.

Possible Kim, who later became Lesley as Daddy didn't want her named after a dog, and decided to name her after a man instead, gave her mam one of what was going to become one of many of her specialty dirty looks when she heard the news of the name change. Her mam put it down to wind, but was mildly suspicious.

The father of her child, her soon to be husband, Callie, had been away at the time of the baby's birth, dealing with a couple of problems. One, his divorce, and two, the last two weeks of a prison sentence at HMP Strangeways, brought about by his "get rich quick" money making scheme. Or fraud, as the judge called it.

Callie, a handsome young man who'd arrived in the mother country a few years earlier, was destined to be the love, and the 'hate' of her life. He and Joyce had met at the Ritz in town. They had been inseparable ever since that fateful meeting.

Mixed relationships were frowned upon in those days. Callie and Joyce didn't care; they'd meet whatever problems when they came. They were in love and now they were parents, parents who were now being encouraged to part from each other and their baby.

Baby carried on having her dinner, while listening to those women, all dressed in the same frocks, rabbiting on, all about illegitimate blah blah and ruining your life.

Then it was a visit from God's first birthday present, the grandparents. After being cooed and awwed over, she burped, and closed her eyes. *I'd better remember all this. It may make a good book,* she thought, as she drifted off to sleep.

CHAPTER ONE
THE EARLY DAYS

So, there I was. Ten days old and already hitting the bottle.

The 60's were tough, and the 60's in Manchester, even tougher.

Me mam was having some problems too, and I don't mean rubber rings and stitches either. Not only was she an Unwed Mother, cue screeching violins and close up on face, but the hospital staff had their suspicions that my father was not from 'round these parts.' Cue close up on baby's face. Deadpan.

"She'll be a burden to you. MISS Holden." How prophetic!

"How will you live?" No such thing as 'Income Support' in those days. Women usually stayed home while men were the 'breadwinners,' and if the breadwinner was doing 'porridge,' well, you were a tad buggered.

"Let me give you a bit of advice, chuck. Why don't you let us put her in a nice 'home' far, far away, and you can pretend this never happened, and who knows? One day you might meet and get married to a nice 'local' man. Someone you can have REAL children with, if you know what I mean." *What was I? A doll?*

Suddenly, the door bursts open and there stand Batman and Robin! Or as I came to know them, Nana and Granddad.

"Never you mind how she's going to 'live'." Nana shot the trademark dirty look, which I was to use to great effect in the coming years, at the nurse.

"We'll support her!"

I thought she just said they shouldn't mind? Nana continued her rant. "And as for putting MY grandchild in a HOME ... A HOME? A HOME?"

When she was angry, she repeated herself. Loudly. "The ONLY HOME this Baby is going to is, number (not tellin' cos I don't want all me fans flockin' there plaguing the new tenants for memorabilia) soddin' Romney Street. Isn't that right 'r Bob?"

"Yes, dear," said 'Robin.'

"Right come on 'r Joyce. Get your stuff together and let's get out of this place." Her comment was accompanied by a glance so withering Bette Davis would have hamstrung Joan Crawford, just to get to Nana first, for lessons. It hadn't been easy for Nana and Granddad to make the decision to support Mam. They were of their time and had been greatly hurt at her getting pregnant before marriage, and positively apoplectic at her being with a 'coloured' man. In all fairness Nana wasn't really 'mithered'. She herself was the daughter of a Russian Jewish émigré and a Yorkshire lass. But Granddad? Well Granddad was a Victorian! He was born in 1886. He was 29 years older than Nana. But not so you'd notice, except in his views on 'Other Races'.

"A Bloody WOG? She's courting a WOG? What the bloody hell have you been doing to her Flo? I'n't it bad enough, YOU coming from bloody Yorkshire and the Russian Front? It's them bloody films at the Adephi. I told you to keep an eye on her when she kept asking them daft questions."

"Dad?"

"Yes, pet?"

"Why are the coloured people always the maids and butlers?"

"Because that's the way it is, pet."

"But why can't they be the other people, too? Like the bosses and the lovely ladies?"

"Flo, pass us a match for me pipe. Do you want an ice-cream 'r Joyce, before the interval's over?"

If you can't answer a question, change the subject. That's how it went in our family.

But, several years later, here they were, coming to the rescue of the daughter who had 'shamed' them. Who had caused divisions in the extended family.

"If you ever let her over your doorstep again, me and you are finished as brother and sister."

I never ever met any of Granddad's brothers and sisters, so you can work out for yourself how THAT threat went down with him.

None of that mattered though, because of two things.

Mam was an only child therefore severely limiting their choice in grandchildren.

But mainly, it was because when they saw me, any prejudice, ill-feeling towards Mam or racial stereotype, went out the window.

4

They saw me and I was perfect, the best grandchild they could ever have been given.

I saw them, and the feeling was mutual.

All in all, it appears I was born into 'turbulent' times, amidst a backdrop of racial tensions.

No wonder I drank!

* * *

Two buses later and here I was, all snuggled up in my pram, pushed up against the sideboard in the back room of our house in Romney Street, Moston, snoozing contentedly in the house that was to bring so much fun and happiness to my life, with the people who were to raise and nurture me, and guide me along the pathway of life. *To this day, the little boy in "Baa Baa Black Sheep" lives on Moston Lane.*

Let battle commence ...

I was spoilt rotten as an only grandchild, and didn't have to share them at all for the first two years of my life.

Then, Mam and Dad decided I needed a playmate and sister number two came along. I could tell you some stories about her, the original 'Damian' in a skirt. Quickly followed, and I mean quick, by sisters number three and four. Then, da-da-da-dah, her son. I'll tell you about him in Chapter 6. And finally, sister number five. Me mam constantly had 'sick' on her for the first eight years of her marriage, and I being her firstborn and witness to all these new arrivals, was convinced she was fat. It took me years to get the connection between big tummies and babies. Innocent times. If she wasn't boiling stew, she was boiling nappies. That's diapers, if you're reading this on the other side of The Pond.

Now I know what you're thinking nowadays reader, as you scroll down on your Kindle.

She was two weeks old, how could she possibly remember all that now?

What can I say?

I'm a Mancunian. We learn quickly. We are blessed with Northern Wit, and we don't forget a kindness or a 'slight'. There's a saying, probably made up by a Manc. 'On the sixth day, God made Manchester.' That says it all. Don't ask me to define 'Mancunian' because I can't. Wikipedia may help you with that. *I just know.* There's something in us that makes us see the 'funny' side of life.

And boy, can I tell you some funny stories about my family. In the following chapters I'm going to introduce you to the characters and the community that contributed to my northern life and taught me that there's always something in a 'bad situation' that you can get a laugh out of. And that is as close as I can get to explain being Mancunian, without the use of props.

I loved my northern life. And, it was about to get a lot more crowded. But, the bigger the cast, the better the entertainment, or so they say (though I've not got a clue who 'they' are).

I'll introduce you properly, to the grown-ups first.

CHAPTER TWO
THE GROWN-UPS

My dad was what they call nowadays 'a player'. Or as my mam put it, 'a cheating dog'. A handsome man indeed, but that's just my humble opinion. Wonderful father, terrible husband, though having said that, he was Mam's one and only love. They met, married and stayed married till death did them part. That's the way it was in those days.

When he passed, Mam sighed and said, "I thought we'd have more time. There was so much more to say."

"Like what, Mam?" I asked tenderly.

"Well I'm not talking about his contribution to world peace, the cheating tw*t," she replied.

"Oh, Mam. Why didn't you just divorce him?"

"WHAT! And make him happy, are you MAD?"

That was Mam all over. Weird but normal, practical but daft, loving, yet capable of committing murder.

A true Mancunian was Mam. She was the reason that, many years later, I tried to dissuade one of my many sisters from naming her son, Sol.

"You know she's gonna call him 'r Sol, don't ya?"

"Well, I'm not passing up the opportunity for THAT comedy gold." She did it as well. She called him Sol. It was worth it!

"Oy, arsehole! Your nana's calling you."

Me mam, working class, through and through: "I'm not getting sterilised in case you lot get run over by a bus."

A BUS? Can't we have something a bit posher, like a plane crash, or at the very least a car?

Me mam. A product of her 'time'. Impervious to political correctness, not that it had been invented then.

She called us, 'half-caste' (still does). But we give her dirty looks when *Roots* is on ... fair do's!

Me mam. Honest as the day is long. Doesn't owe no one nowt, and knows how much she's got in the bank to the nth degree. "What sort of idiot goes overdrawn? How can you eat two apples if you've only got one?" *There's a mad logic in there somewhere.*

Me mam. The type of woman who sends cards on behalf of the dog.

Congratulations on the birth of your baby. Lots of love, Pepper!

The most private person I know. But, give her 10 minutes at the bus stop and the whole queue knows every mistake I ever made in life. Along with my age, how long she'd been in labour with me, and how my dad is a cheating bugger!

Me mam. A founding member of the Manchester Operatic Society. The 'madder' she got the higher the voice rose. When she was fuming, crystal glasses were in severe danger. Her soprano meant trouble!

Me mam. I just love her so much. Do I tell her?

Don't be daft! She's not mithered with all that rubbish. Does she know I love her?

You bet! I think? *Oo-er.*

And when she and Dad got together, well, it was 'moider' as they say in *Hart to Hart.*

A lethal combination, love and loathing in one package. Every day brought a new drama. But I wouldn't have had it any other way, and do you know what? In the days before video games and the Internet, their rows were our entertainment. The rest of the street's, too. Dad would never hit a woman and Mam had a terrible aim. So no one got physically hurt.

One time they had a massive row and Dad left for a while. Mam's best mate took up residence in our house. Her job was to 'tut' and give Dad 'daggers' when he came to see us. Anyway, one day a man with a briefcase came. Mam took him in the kitchen and closed the door.

I remember it well; it was the day of the Englebert Crumpledick marathon record session. All day, and I mean ALL, she'd been playing *There Goes My Everything*. I think it was on its 96th airing when the suit man turned up. But to be honest I'd lost count and the will to live at the 25th. Five minutes after the Suit Man left, she strode up to the Stereogram and put on *Please Release Me*. I know they say a change is as good as a rest, but *puh-leeze.*

Still, she who pays the leccy bill controls the turntable (her words not mine).

"When you've got money for a Dansette, then you can play Pinky and Perky till the cows come home. But whilst we're waiting, I'M playing Englebert." And with that, she walked out of the room. There was a glint in her eye, as she went back in the kitchen, that I would not come to understand until I was married and cheated on myself. I suppose you could define it as evil. Muttering something under her breath about 'maintenance,' she had practically shimmied out the room.

Sometime later, after she had forgiven me for having the audacity to look like him: "Stop looking at me with that face. You look just like him."

Well, pardon ME for saving you from a potential DNA test. But I digress! Anyway, she sat me down and told me that Dad was working away and asked if I wanted to see him.

"Ooh yes please, where is he working?"

"Erm, in a pawnshop."

"Like Mays," *our local pawnshop* said I, excitedly. I loved going to Mays with Mam, she went nearly every week.

I think she used to lend them her wedding rings to make the shop look pretty. There were lots of pretty things in there.

The day came and we set off on the bus. We were only on it for five minutes and we got off at the Empire State Building. OK, it was really called the Cooperative Building Society Building, known locally as the CIS, but allow me a little glamour.

Up the road we marched. I can't exactly remember what street it was, but there were definitely no houses there, because Mam never once said, "Look at the state of them nets, I wouldn't give the dog a cup of tea from that hovel."

As you'll find out, me mam was a bit of a snob.

In front of us loomed a massive brownstone building. We queued up; there were lots of people visiting.

Everyone in the world must work here, I remember thinking.

Soon we were led into my dad's office. It was just like Mays 'cept no jewels. There was a big brown counter with bars, and Dad was behind it. We had a lovely visit ... well I did. Mam sat there doing the 'huffy' face we had come to accept as normal for her.

I didn't realise it at the time, but in future years I was able to tell my own children the story of how Mam sent Dad to prison for not paying child support.

Happy days indeed!

Then there was my nana. The tree that sprouted the branch that grew the apple that became me.

Everything me mam was, snobby, quiet, strict, she was NOT. Oh, don't get me wrong. Mam was a loving woman, but she had to deal with the day to day practicalities. She showed her love for us by feeding, clothing and not mislaying us anywhere. Nana showed her love by lifting up her skirt to show off her 'bloomers' and leading us in a chorus of *Sally* by Gracie Fields.

"Sallllleeeeeeeee, sallleeeeeee ... pride of the allllllleeeeeeeee."

She met my granddad, 30 years her senior, when she was in service at the doctor's surgery, next door but one, at Romney Street, Moston. *I'd rather be an old man's darlin' than a young man's slave* was her mantra for life. Granddad was a widower living alone with his young daughter, having lost his first wife to consumption two years earlier. Nana told me she felt proper sorry for him because in those days it wasn't seen as right for a man to be left 'holding the baby'. She knew how hard it was for him having to work and look after a child, so she used to leave a bowl of something or the other on the doorstep. I think she cooked her way into his heart. A talent my mam didn't inherit. Oh my God, that STEW! I'll tell you more about that later.

Anyway, fast forward a few years through marriage, the birth of me mam and the arrival of me. We find ourselves in the swinging 60's. Nana. Forever clothed in a wraparound 'pinny' and a turban, except for 'high days and holidays' when she wore a wig with a hat attached, and took the 'pinny' off. Very scary!

She had a friend *and I say that reservedly* called 'Alice the Malice'. Just Alice really, but you'll come to understand! Alice had a 'weepy eye' and her dog, some kind of poodle crossed with a scruffy git, had a matching weepy eye too! Honest to God I'm not making a word of this up!

Between them, they could destroy the character of half of Moston on no more than a pot of tea and two egg custards. "Did you see the state of her at number 22, and if that's his child I'm the Sheikh of Araby."

On and on they chattered about people I couldn't put a face to. Whilst I sat, like the perfect child I was, playing with me nana's button tin and absolutely NOT listening in to the grown-ups. Just waiting patiently for someone else to pop round, as they often did. And then it happened. Mrs Charlton from Bluebell Avenue (the posh houses) passed by.

My nana used to 'do' for her. More on that subject later.

Three of them in one room. Sooner or later, one of them would have to be the first to go.

That's when the 'daggers' would come out, "Ooh did you see the state of what she had on?" And for me? Another lesson in life learned. Well two really. Never be the first one to leave a bunch of gossiping women and even more importantly: Bessie Charlton's son was Jesus!

Apparently he was born whilst Mr. Charlton was away for three years fighting the war.

"A bleedin' immaculate conception," me nana said.

Throughout all this, my lovely gentle granddad kept quiet.

A wise man was me granddad. Knew when to keep his mouth shut. Which was mostly all the time. There was no getting away from it. The Women of the family most definitely ruled the roost.

Granddad was the silent type though. But when he did get the chance, he taught me some great things. How to clean a pipe, how to reach the light switch with a stick, how many senna pods make the perfect help-you-to-poo drink, and which football team to support. We were Blues. I still am. CTID.

But mainly he taught me about his favourite subject, the war, and as it turned out, the wrong bloody one!

"When you go home," the teacher at St. James Primary School *Junior 2* said, "find out what your grandparents did in the war and prepare a little talk to give to class." I felt sorry for the lad who sat at my table, John Schmidt. *That bit's a lie! I was the most foreign person in my class and even then I was only half-foreign!*

To be honest, like I just said, Granddad LOVED to talk about the war. So I already knew lots about his adventures. He never blinkin' shut up about it! But what I hadn't realised was that the war HE'D been talking about, had been the FIRST World War.

That's a May/December romance for ya! Confuses us grandkids. No wonder Alice the Malice *Nana's aforementioned friend of many faces ... TWO!* got upset when she asked me to guess what famous war song she had danced to at her wedding.

"Go on," she snarled. "You're a little Miss know-it-all. Have a guess?"

"Erm ... It's A Long Way To Tippertary?" *That's how I pronounced it!*

"Did you hear that, Flo? The cheeky madam!"

Nana had been in the middle of putting out the tea when Alice had barged in. Nana never locked the door till last thing. You could do that in them days. So people just came and went all day long with not a single knock. She pretended to be rearranging the 'Prem'. But I knew she was trying not to laugh.

Anyway, back to this school assignment. Like I said, I knew the ins and outs of a cat's collar when it came to Granddad and the war, from Day One to the Armistice. Remember, me mam was an only child. That made me (for two years and one month) an ONLY grandchild. He had all the time in the world to introduce and instruct me in the delights of warfare. I found out that in World War II, he'd been in the Home Guard and me nana had worked in a factory making parts for bombs. Every time you see a picture of a bombed out Berlin, say to yourself, "My nana did that." The next week, I gave my little talk at school. Don't really remember much about it, except Mr. Cole giving me a funny look when I said my granddad had been a bit too young for the Boer War so was really excited about the next one.

Despite the thirty year age gap, Nana and Granddad were a match made in Heaven. Kind of like Mam and Dad, but without the arguments.

* * *

Oh yeah! I mentioned before about my nana 'doing' for Mrs Charlton.

Nana 'did' for quite a few people. She was a cleaning lady extraordinaire. Sometimes as a special treat she'd let me go with her. Except when she 'did' the Ben Brierley.

Never got the logic behind that. A kid can hang about OUTSIDE a pub at the risk of getting 'patted' on the head by drunks a bloomin' million times. *Mind you, nowadays, you might get stabbed or shot!* But she can't wait at the end of the bar?

"Good girls don't go in pubs," Nana told me once.

"You do!"

I could be cheekier to Nana. She never got 'nowty'. Mam could learn a thing or two from her!

"I'll tell you about pubs when you get bigger. Now get your coat on. You can come with me to Mrs Charlton's."

Mrs Charlton, AKA Queen Snooty, Elizabeth (Bessie) Charlton. No relation at all to the 'Athletic' Charltons. The woman was permanently attached to her Parker Knoll! I dreamed of having a go on that wondrous moving chair that magically turned into a bed. But NO! There she was, week in, week out, glued to it. Selfish mare!

And every time I went, whilst Nana 'did', she'd say the exact same thing to me.

"See that picture on the wall?"

You couldn't bloody miss it. She had an arrangement of plastic ferns and furry plastic fruit draped round it. 'Orrible!

"Yes Mrs Charlton." *I was such a goody two shoes, and two-faced!*

"That's the Queen, that is. Got the same name as me. I met her once."

You were passing the Town Hall on a bus in the days before your Cyril got the Morris Minor, and she was there opening something.

Blank stare from me. What am I supposed to say? It's not even a proper story. No punch line or sense in it at all. I make a non-committal grunt which I can pass off as anything. Yes/No/Ooh really? How amazing.

She gives me a funny look and checks her hearing aid. It's full of wax which she wipes on her monogrammed but still snotty hanky.

"Would you like a sweet?"

God no!

"Do they have sweets in your country?" *What a stupid cow. How many times does my nana have to tell her my dad is from abroad, I was born HERE?*

I make a little groan. She thinks I've said yes.

"Pass me my handbag. The one I got from Kendal's. Frightfully expensive I'll tell you, Flo, but 'r Cyril *you just can't take the common out of some people. No matter how hard they try*, says 'aim werthit'."

Nana gives a little grunt and goes back to mangling the crocheted doily. I'm planning to 'mangle' sister number three's fingers in Nana's mangle, as soon as I can get her alone. But that's another story.

I've returned with the bag. I know what's coming next.

She 'roots' through the bag and brings out ... a barley sugar!

That's NOT sweets! That's medicine! Old people have barley sugars, poorly people have barley sugars. I want a sherbet dip and some mojos.

It's gone sticky too, and has a bit of a Steradent tablet stuck to it. At least I'll get clean teeth!

"Go on take it. I can see you want to."

I'm a great actress!

"Thank you."

I pretend to put it in my mouth and move towards the 'classy' tribute to Her Majesty.

"You look a bit like the Queen, Mrs Charlton." *Am a proper 'creep' when I want to be.*

"So people say," replies 'Snooty Knickers'. Gawd, what a deluded woman. A poodle perm does not a Queen make. *Yes Nana! I heard you and Alice the Malice gossiping.*

I place the 'sweet' behind a bit of fern. It sticks perfectly.

I STILL hate barley sugars to this day. Can still taste that yuckiness, especially when I'm wandering down Moston Lane and I pass her old house. I come over all funny and have to walk past quickly. But Moston itself, except for that bit, is a place I absolutely love.

CHAPTER THREE
MAYHEM IN MOSTON

There I am sat on the kitchen table. Me, Mam and sometimes Dad, he gets about, are still living with Nana and Granddad.

We've lived in the odd few other places; Moss Side, Whalley Range. But Dad has been known to 'gamble' away the rent money. So Mam says she's not going anywhere until she gets a Corporation House with HER name on the rent book.

There's another kid as well, 'r Karin, and Mam is looking fat again.

But back to me!

Like I just said, there I am perched precariously on the big wooden table that doubles as a wash stand. Top half done. Bottom half waiting and then, The Bachelors' *I Believe* comes on the radio. Lovely song, 'till me nana decides to sing along with it, from start to finish.

Good job it's a short song. I'm bloody freezing up here on the most ginormous table I'd ever seen in my three long years on this earth.

She's not exactly blessed in the singing department either. Just think Hilda Ogden, but not as tuneful.

Even though the song has stopped and some idiot is waffling on, "Now then, now then guys and gals." Nana is still swaying. She's rubbing me dry at the same time. Ouch! That towel is rough.

"I beleeeeeeve ... ee ah 'r Lesley."

Try saying that after a pint of 'Boddies'. "Lovely lads them Bachelors. Brothers you know, I'd 'brother' them!"

Nana! I'm THREE for 'Pete's' sake. He's one of Billy Eck's mates. Never met a one of them me whole life.

"Lovely Irish Brogue, don't you think?"

I'm THREE! I'm still developing my own dropped aitches and eee-arrrs. How am I supposed to have an opinion on regional dialects?

"Stop talking daft 'r Flo," pipes up my granddad. "She's only a little mite. She doesn't understand a word you're saying. Come here darling. Let Granddad tell you all about the war!"

I hadn't even noticed Granddad sat in his chair next to the fire. Mind you, there was also the maiden and a massive tin bath blocking me view.

"Oh shut up 'r Bob. There's more to life than the bloody war. Got us through the blackouts did a good old sing-song."

The way these two go on, sometimes, I think my only option as a grown-up will be to become a singing soldier. Right, Hitler. You're DEAD! But first, let's have a chorus of *White Cliffs of Dover*.

She mustn't like the next song because I've got her undivided attention now and half a tub of Johnson's Baby Powder between my legs.

"I don't want my little precious getting chapped legs. Come on, chuck. Let's get you down from there. Why don't you go and play in your mam's room till dinner's ready."

Just so you know, In the North, we eat dinner in the daytime. The posh lot calls it lunch. We ain't posh. We are normal.

Me nana makes lovely dinners. Me mam doesn't! Mam's 'stew' became legendary for its awfulness. In years to come, I finally found a use for it as a teaching aid cum punishment for my own kids.

"If you don't stop doing that I'm taking you to me mam's"

"Hurrah!"

"She's making stew."

"I've stopped!"

Anyway, back to me nana's singing, for want of a better word. Oh it's OK, I've found one. Caterwauling. I knew that junior dictionary would come in handy one day. She certainly wasn't shy when it came to 'belting out' a number. Unfortunately, she certainly couldn't 'carry a tune' either. Her version of Gracie Fields' *Sally* was legendary and almost painful. *Vowel sounds really 'carry' up North. She 'murdered' Edith Piaf YEARS before the woman actually died!*

But being related to her, I must have gotten used to it. I came to love my nana's singing. OK, tolerate, and she taught me loads of songs. I still know all the words to *A Bicycle Built for Two*, and many others.

Me mam, *Hyacinth Bucket, in her 20's*, wasn't best pleased though, when I started belting out: *Is your daughter any better than she ought to be* whilst she was deciding between a sideboard and a kitchen cabinet in the furniture shop.

"Mam! Stop teaching the kids rude songs. She's just mortified me in Beddoes!"

"OH shurrup 'r Joyce."

Innit funny when nanas tell mams off?

"I don't know where you get all them 'airs and graces' from. It certainly isn't from me."

She was right about that! Me nana and poshness were total strangers. But that's why I loved her so much. There's nowt wrong with the 'common touch', but it was hard sometimes to believe she was my mam's mam.

It's also hard to believe that mams were once kids too. I mean, I used to look at mine and think: there is no way you've EVER had fun, 'cos if you did, you'd understand me a bit more. But NO! You've got to have RULES and more rules.

The biggest rule was 'If it's fun you can't do it'!

Having said that, I came to accept, if not completely understand, that most mams WERE kids at one time. Even MINE and I know that because Nana told me. Nanas NEVER lie to kids. *The rent man is a different thing though!*

"Oh, come in Eddie ... me knees are playing up something awful and I've not had time to go to the post office."

She's been to bingo, and lost. "Want a cup of tea, pet?"

"Go on then, Flo. So what do you know?"

God, he's gonna be here all day.

"Waffle, waffle ... her at number 43, blah, blah ... no better than she ought to be."

"Hold on a minute, Eddie. Little people in the room, if you know what I mean?"

I swear she thinks I'm Helen Keller sometimes.

I can see you looking at me, Nana, doing that nodding thing with your head, like Joey the budgie does.

"Why don't you go and play in your mam's bedroom, 'r Lesley?"

"OK, Nana." The walls are paper thin anyway. I'll still hear every word they're saying. Up the stairs I go. It's like climbing Mount Everest, only steeper. We don't have a banister just some rope to hold on to. Like me granddad says: "Banisters are for Nancys." *Nope, don't know who she is either, but I'm guessing she's on intimate terms with Billy Eck.*

It's alright for Granddad, though, to say banisters don't matter. He's got a 'funny' leg, *I never get the 'joke'!*, and sleeps in the front room, where we set the jelly for the trifle on Sundays. I'll tell you one thing. Me granddad's got some will power. Put me in a room all night with a jelly and only one of us is coming out of there!

Mam's bedroom is still exactly the same as when she was (allegedly) young.

Nana and Granddad used to mark the wall each year on her birthday. What a shorty!

The walls are painted with pink paint. It's called 'Distemper' and I know why. Every time you touch it your clothes get dusty and it puts mams in a 'temper' 'cos they have to wash your clothes for the 'umpteenth' time.

There are pictures on the wall of 'old' people she used to like.

Victor Mature dressed as 'Samson' *eww!*, Frankie Vaughn *eww-er!*

She definitely likes 'em tall and dark. Me poor dad never had a chance! But I have to count my blessings. I could have been 'Lesley Humperdinck'.

That would have gone down well on the streets of Collyhurst!

"Humperdinck? You STINK! Stink, stink, stinky, stink, stink. *Brilliant lyrics!*

I can hear Nana in full throttle downstairs.

"So I said to 'r Bob," *Call him by his proper name, Woman! ... It's Granddad!* "that Gladys Birchall and soap are strangers. The bottom of my shoes are cleaner than her Wotsit."

It was a long time before I found out what a 'Wotsit' referred to, and to this day I can't eat a Cheesy one!

I've snuck to the top of the stairs now, so I can hear better. A bit risky I know. But don't worry dear reader. There's no way I'm getting caught, 'cos the stairs are in a 'cupboard'. That's RIGHT ... you have to open a door and the stairs are behind it. The door handle sticks too. If she tries to catch me out, by the time she's opened it, I'm back whistling nonchalantly on me mam's divan.

"You alright, pet? You seem out of breath."

"No I'm fine Nana. I was just sat sitting here ... for ages ... never moved ...

just reading Mam's old magazines. Very good article here on Rock Hudson ... 'He's ALL Man'. Couldn't hear a thing! Did you want me?"

My propensity for 'fibbing' is starting to worry me.

I can see where me mam got the 'LOOK' from. For a second or two, she stares at me in that 'methinks somebody's telling porkies, where's the belt?' kind of way.

Then she remembers she's not a mam she's a nana.

"Eee arr luv, I brought you up the button tin and a packet of Rolos. I'm just having another cup of tea with Eddie, then I'll do ham butties and an egg custard for your tea."

I LOVED my nana. Best nana in the world.

Nothing like me mam. But here's the funny thing. Years later when I had babies of my own, did the woman not have a complete personality change? Got my kids completely fooled, with her 'Nanarish' ways.

It must be catching, 'cos now I've turned into HER! I'm Doomed! *And so are me kids.*

Speaking of kids, I think you should meet some of my siblings. After all, they helped 'ruin' me childhood too, bloomin' clingy gets!

I'll start with number two 'r Karin.

Karin came along two years and one month after me. A short, and in my opinion, SPITEFUL child, she is now a lovely woman and sister. She's still short though.

She was responsible for me getting the blame, when SHE did it. On more than one occasion.

I'd share a fond memory from our childhood if I could. But you'll just have to make do with a memory ...

When I was quite young, I decided I wanted to become a hairdresser. It was a dream that lasted until I saw Audrey Hepburn in *A Nun's Story*.

After that revelation, anytime me mam was looking for a tea towel she didn't have to look further than my head.

"For the MILLIONTH time, get my bloody towel off your head."

"It's a wimple. I want to be a nun when I grow up, and it's a sin to exaggerate." *Pious look on face.*

"When I see a nun wearing a dress with the words 'Greetings from Blackpool' printed all over it I'll believe THAT is a nun's hat."

Heathen.

"Until then, it's a tea towel, so for the 67th time, Julie Andrews. Oh! Is that precise enough to save me from hell and damnation? Get the soddin' towel off your head. "

She'll be sorry when I'm Joan of Arc.

But back to the 'hairdressing'. No doll was safe. Tiny Tears looked like she'd been electrocuted! And I'd had a terrible accident with Cindy and me mam's 'Dolly Blue', who should have been sued, ('cept no one had heard of 'suing' in them days) for false advertising.

WHO wouldn't think 'Dolly Blue' was a hair dye for 'DOLLS' of a 'certain age'?

Like me nana's friend 'blue rinse' Beryl.

"Us ladies of a certain age need all the help we can get," she says gawking in me nana's mirror and touching up her bright red lipstick.

She looks like a toddler who's just ate a jam doughnut. She does this weird thing where she 'hutches' up her boobs. *Think Les Dawson, only uglier.* And even weirder, when she does it, me nana and any other woman in the room, does it too!

I won't go anywhere near 'em. I'm not catching that!

So, anyway, having run out of dolls, I only had one other option, a sister!

"Come 'ere 'r Karin. Do you want me to make you look like a princess?"

"Go on then."

Easy!

"Sit down then, and put this cape round your neck."

It took ages to destroy that umbrella, and anyway why would Mam need an umbrella in Manchester? It's not like she was in a hurry to meet Dr Foster in Gloucester. She could buy a new one.

"OK modom." Snip, snip here, snip, snip there. (Whoops copyright!) A bit off this side, a bit off that side. A bit more off this side, a 'tad' off the other. OH MY GOD!

"Ere, put this bonnet on."

"Why?"

"'Cos it's FASHION, and don't take it off till we've gone to bed. I'll let you lick some of me sherbet dip ... OK?"

"OK" *Thank God she's simple.*

Me mam, at 1 o'clock:

"Aw doesn't 'r Karin look cute in that bonnet?"

At 3 o'clock:

"Have you still got your bonnet on luv? Aw, bless her."

At 5 o'clock:

"Right, time to take that bonnet off now, luv. You need to get some air to your ears, and it's almost time to get ready for bed."

At 5:01

"Where is she?"

"I'm gonna KILL HER! LESLEY DONNA MARIA MOTTLEY!" *All my names, and in capitals too. This is death penalty serious.* "Come here right now and explain your sister's head!" *Will somebody hurry up and invent Childline?*

Thank God Nana and Granddad saw the funny side. They calmed Mam down. Her bark was always worse than her bite. Life went on, and Karin's hair grew back. Eventually.

But things were about to change for the inhabitants of Romney Street. We were on the move with Mam and Dad, to the place I was to spend the biggest part of my childhood, Collyhurst, and Nana and Granddad were about to meet, and fall in love with sister number three, 'r 'manda, and you know how they say every family has got one, well I don't specifically know what 'one' was but she was IT.

CHAPTER FOUR
A SISTER OR TWO … OR THREE

As I'm sure you've come to realise, we were a big family. Six kids in eight years. Me mam must have been permanently knackered. But kids cost money and Mam had to go to work in order to finance her having-babies hobby.

By the time she had Amanda, we had moved to 'rooms' in Whalley Range and shortly after that to my beloved Collyhurst. Bills needed to be paid, so the decision was made that Amanda would live with Nana and Granddad for a bit. Dad would work days and Mam would work nights. So they both took turns looking after me and number two.

To be honest, me and number two didn't have a clue what was going on. As long as we were fed, watered and allowed access to *Watch With Mother*, we were happy. We didn't have a clue who Amanda was 'till she turned up one day. *She'd lived with Nana and Granddad for the first seven months of her life.* A big fat thing, taking up space in OUR room.

Immediately we began work on getting rid! It didn't work though. She's still about. A lovely woman, I have to say. But what an obnoxious child!

So, out comes the Silver Cross pram again! And there's fairy elephant sat sitting in it, taking up space and room in Mam and Dad's affections.

Me and number two were gutted. Number two took it harder though. I'd already experienced the feeling of being usurped, when she'd bloody arrived a year earlier, with a kiss curl on top of her head to conceal the 666 tattoo.

Mam kept her eye on us though. The woman had extra eyes too. She'd even told us where they were.

"I've got eyes in the back of my head. So you two be careful. I'm watching you."

God, it was hard to get away with stuff with her about. But now and again opportunity knocked, and we didn't need Hughie Green to tell us to 'have a go'. Nope! We were daft enough to just go for it!

"OK kids we're off to Nana's." *Hurrah.*

"Lesley and Karin, have you got knickers on?"

No, Mother. We thought we'd show you up and go commando.

"Yes Mam. Can we go now?"

"In a minute. I'm just putting me scarf on." *That doesn't take a minute, she'll be titivating it for the next hour.* She senses our unrest.

"Ee-ar, why don't you wait at the door and rock 'r 'manda's pram?" *It's my bloomin' pram. I had it first.* "Don't go near the steps though." We were still in Whalley Range at this time. Our house had a million steps (OK, six) leading up to the front door. Mam called them 'buggers'.

"It's murder getting a pram up and down these buggers. Did that not occur to you Callie?"

Me dad just replied in his laid back way, "You wanted a house. I got you a house." *Actually 2 rooms, but we didn't know that at the time. We thought the whole thing was ours.*

So me and Karin sat on the top step, gently rocking the pram. With our feet.

Karin was playing with the brake, lifting it up and snapping it down. Great fun when you're three.

The part of me that was a Goody Two Shoes kicked in.

"Don't do that. Mam said we're not to ever touch the brake 'cos it's dangerous."

If I could have read minds, I'd have bet money on what me sister was thinking. *Who gives a s**t?* She was always a rebel, and hard-faced.

Those curls and that 'butter wouldn't melt' expression were just cunning disguises. Number two was Damian before anyone had heard of *The Omen*.

I must have had my attention diverted by something going on up the street, because I turned away for a moment and next thing all I heard was 'bumpity bump bump THUD'!

The pram wasn't at the top of the steps any more. But the mam was!

"Oh my God. What have you done to my child?" *Why is she looking at me?*

I swear she jumped the whole of the steps at once. The pram was on its side. Mam put it right way up and pulled Amanda out of it. *She'd better check it for damage. Amanda's a chunky child. She's probably put a dint in it, and by the look of Mam, she's gonna need it again.*

"Thank God she's alive." *Drama queen!*

"Right you! Come here." *WHY is she only talking to me? There's another kid here too.*

"It weren't me, Mam. I didn't do it. Our Karin was playing with the brake. She did it."

"And you just watched her?" *I can't bloody win.* "You're the eldest. I told you to watch your sisters."

"I was watching 'em."

"Yeah, watching 'em die."

Karin just smirked. Unless Mam was looking at her, then she did that angelic simpering which always seemed to work for her. The cow! Honest to God that kid got away with murder, well almost!

Amanda wasn't even hurt. The combination of a pram built like a tank, twenty-six blankets and the piles of fat round her belly were enough to save her. Still, there'd be plenty more attempts on her life during the early years. Luckily she survived, and if the truth be told, I did come to love her in time. But I held her responsible back then for my first clip round the ear hole. I craved vengeance, and was able to find many opportunities, and more than a sore earhole as the consequence. But hey! I'm a risk-taker. When an opportunity to make a sibling suffer arose I was in like Flynn. Which reminds me of a time, just a year or two later ... God gave Amanda the gift of naivety. A 'two for the price of one' gift in my eyes! That girl would believe ANYTHING.

Picture the scene:

We've moved to Collyhurst by now. *Second floor flat, more about that later in the book.*

It's the summer holidays. It's raining. (This IS Manchester!) The only thing on the telly is me mam's blown glass fish. *In later years I snapped its tail off, but Amanda got the blame, so no probs there.* The three of us are sat on the landing. Bored. To. Death. Me mam (theirs too) is either doing something in the kitchen or being pregnant. We daren't let HER know we're bored 'cos she'll start coming out with some nonsense 'bout tidying bedrooms. *That is NOT entertainment Mother!* What can we do?

I KNOW!

"Do you know, 'manda, that when you were staying at Nana's, the people who make parks came here and put that slide in."

"What slide?"

"That one, there, at the end of the landing. Can't you see it"?

Now the blessing was that someone had recently nicked the pull out bit of the rubbish chute. It was easier than I thought to convince her. *Thank you thief.*

"OH WOW," she says. RESULT!

"So who wants first go?"

I'll tell you now; Amanda was the Usain Bolt of 'hand putting up for first goes'. "OK fair do's, 'manda goes first." (Insert Dick Dastardly's evil laugh.)

Like I just said, we lived on the 2nd floor.

Sister number two runs down the stairs to wait at the bottom of the shaft, and I help (?!) 'r 'manda to get on the 'slide'. I push, we wait. "Is she there yet?" I shout.

"NO!"

We both run, me down, sister number two up! We meet on the 1st floor. We can hear a gentle sobbing, which soon becomes a panicked scream. *Oh my goad! She's such a DRAMA QUEEN.*

We look at each other, and both run upstairs.

"MAM! 'manda's stuck in the chute. We told her NOT to do it." *Please let God be busy saving African children. Surely he can't see EVERYTHING.*

I don't recall much else about that day. I was taken ill with a sore backside and stayed in my room. I remember the sound of fire engines though. And the next day she was there, so it couldn't have been that bad.

Another time as I recall, number three was the cause of me getting yet another telling off. Well, that's the way I saw it.

There we were sat in the bedroom. Number three's cot was in it by now, so space was limited. It was winter. No central heating back then, but Mam had put on the oil heater to warm up the room and had just nipped downstairs to get our supper bottles. *Milk not beer.*

I was never one for cuddly toys, but Nana and Grandad must have bought out every teddy in Woolworths for 'r 'manda when she was living with them. *No wonder she was a spoilt cow, they spoilt 'er.*

And the buggers were taking up every inch of MY playing space.

I booted a couple out of the way. It's not like they had feelings, but it made Amanda cry, ha-ha.

"Shut up, whingy knickers ... watch. I'm gonna throw your Donald Duck to the moon."

The brat won't shut up, but she can't get out of the cot to do anything and me and 'r Karin's laughter is covering up the noise of her crying anyway.

"I won't be long," the mam shouts, "I can hear you lot laughing. That's right. Play nice."

Well, Donald was certainly launched. But he didn't reach the moon. He got as far as the oil heater where he became wedged in the front grill. Almost as funny.

I continued setting out my jigsaw. I was always the intellectual one.

"Is Mam making toast?" piped up number two. I sniffed the air.

"I think so," I replied not quite concentrating. I was trying to find Noddy's Bell, and it wasn't a corner piece. This jigsaw was tough; twenty pieces. *I kid you not.*

"Are you smoking 'r Lesley? Aw I'm gonna tell."

"What are you talking about, you horrible likkle midget?" I hated being interrupted when I was concentrating. "I'm a kid, kids can't smoke."

"Well you are."

"What?" I'd been sat with my back to the heater, warming my bum. When I turned round, the heater had somehow turned into a chimney. There was smoke pouring out of it.

I did what any five-and-a-half-year-old child would have done. I panicked and jumped into the nearest haven of safety. That's right, the Cot. Number two jumped in with me and number three just sat there giving us dirty looks. I half expected her to say, "Oy! Second class fares in the back please."

What was it Mam and Dad said to do in a crisis? Oh yeah, hold hands and stick together. Yep, doing that. We heard Mam shout and footsteps coming closer.

"I'm coming now girls. Some bugger's got a bonfire going out there. OH MY GOD! Someone call the fire brigade. My babies, my babies!"

It's amazing how you can realise how much you love someone when you think you're going to lose them. But as soon as you know they are safe and well, you can just turn!

"Are you bloody stupid young lady?" *Yep she's addressing me.* "What sort of idiot just sits there in a cot watching the house burn down?" *A tad dramatic. It was only one room AND only a bit of the carpet ... and Donald Duck got singed.*

We never ever had a portable heater again. Until the advent of affordable central heating, we had to make do with hot water bottles and/or each other to stay warm in bed. I sometimes wonder if that's why she ended up with so many kids.

But for the moment it was just us three, and if I'm honest, I was starting to lose it. The little sods were growing up and challenging my authority. Especially number two. Little Miss Vertically Challenged, or shorta***e, as I called her. She had a birthmark on her elbow. Still does. Now, it's the size of a 1p. Back then it was the size of a McVitie's digestive! Mam called it her 'Beetle'. "It'll stop her being frightened." *Oh yeah, very comforting Mother. A creepy crawly on one's arm!*

She'd recently started waving it in my face in a very threatening manner. Mam was under the illusion that number two was 'cute as a button', but I knew different. Mam saw Shirley Temple, I saw the Tasmanian Devil! So anyway, as time went by, and another sister came into the gang, we became a bit more democratic. No longer could I demand they do what I said. We had to reason. So if for instance, we wanted a late night snack after we had been sent to bed, it wasn't a case of just asking.

Mam's usual bed-time story had become: "I'm sick of the sight of you'se lot. One more peep out of this room, and I'm getting the belt out. Now SHUT UP and go to sleep."

So, the four of us would play 'flee, fly, flo, flum, (Not got a clue what that meant!), to see who was 'it'.

Flippin' eck it's number three. We're doomed before we start.

"What do I say?"

"Just knock on the door and say 'Mam can we have a jam butty?' OK?"

"OK ... 'r Lesley sez can we ..."

"NO NOT 'r LESLEY. Just 'CAN WE HAVE A SODDIN' BUTTY?'"

"Mam'll go mad if I swear."

"I didn't say to swear you stupid ... oh never mind. Repeat after me, 'Can. We. Have. A. Jam. Butty. Please?'"

"I want lemon curd."

(You're not too posh to cosh luv!)

The best way to reduce the odds in this particular battle was to go for the easiest thing to make.

My mam's kitchen was like the local butcher's. Every night at a certain time, everything got washed down and put away, and woe betide the child (usually me) that dared to ask for more. (See Oliver Twist for more details. My life was just like that, with worse food!)

Anyway, back to the 'quick wits' of sister number three. After some intensive training and the use of a motivational tool which involved her 'Tiny Tears' and MY craft scissors, I was fairly confident she'd got it right.

We pushed her out of the bedroom door. She went into the living room and spoke.

"Mam, 'r Lesley stabbed me 'Tiny Tears' in the eye and she said I've got to ask you for jam butties ... and she told me to swear." *The little!!!!*

Silence.

"Can we have jam butties, Mam? But really, I want lemon curd. Can we, can we?"

"Two of youse can!"

God I hated those brats! I needed a break. The school holidays were coming up, so hopefully I'd get a day out or two. Maybe if I could keep Mam occupied with my sparkling wit, she might forget and leave a couple of them on the beach in Rhyl. The one with no sand 'cos that's as much as they deserve, the little horrors. Thank God she had me!

CHAPTER FIVE
ARE WE THERE YET?

A day out with Mam and Dad was a bit of a double-edged sword. On one hand we got to have fun with Dad. On the other Mam was there too with her 'going out kit'.

It contained:

Spare underwear. Obviously childhood incontinence was rife in those days. Times that by the 'Von Trapp' kids, and she needed a bloody massive bag.

Spare socks. In case we dared to get a bit of tar on 'em. Tar was everywhere in them days, and for some reason it was particularly attracted to me.

"I just don't understand that child. She's only been dressed five minutes, and from the front door to the bottom of the landing, she's managed to get covered in tar."

What she didn't know was I was collecting it in the grid under number 54. I'd just been to check it was still there, and was still sticky. The answer to both questions was 'yes'!

Mam was mortified of meeting anyone she knew, if we were any less than pristine.

"I'm not having anyone calling MY kids scruffy. They're half-caste." *What does that have to do with it?* "My kids have got to be twice as clean to be just as clean." *Well, that clears it up!*

Two flannels (one for up, one for down) soaked in a mixture of Dettol and bleach wrapped in a plastic bag. The woman INVENTED baby wipes and didn't even know it!

A handkerchief to spit on in emergencies, such as post-butty trauma.

"Come here 'r whoever, you've got something on your face." *Ewww!*

A mile of spare ribbon, just in case the 100 yards of it you already had on your head came off! There were a lot of 'just in cases' in Mam's life.

"Come here; let me tie that ribbon properly."

"OW! Mam it's too tight."

"Don't talk rubbish. You look lovely." *I feel like my cheeks are where my ears usually go.*

So, back to this particular day out. There we were all togged up like it was Whitsun. *More on that later.* Us lot in the back of Dad's car. (It was a Humber, plenty of room!) Mam and Dad in the front.

"Where are we going, Dad?"

"To Ringway Airport." (Sounds good).

"Are we there yet?" Pipes up number four. We've only gone round the bloody corner. I can still see our roof.

"Is that the Tower?" chirps number three.

"No luv it's an electricity pylon," says Mam. "We're not going to Blackpool darling. Aw Callie, i'n't she cute?"

(I'n't she THICK?!!!)

We motor on for a few more miles. Mam's been quiet for a while. *She's plotting something.* Dad's singing Nat King Cole songs. Tunefully, I may add.

Suddenly she speaks.

"And WHERE were YOU all night?"

Is she MAD? Did he not tuck us up in bed last night? And was he NOT here when we got up this morning? She was probably just looking in the kitchen! We've told her there are OTHER rooms. But will she listen?

Dad just laughs. At least someone finds her funny.

We arrive at the airport. This was the days when the airport was open to loiterers who had no intention of getting on a plane. Nowadays we'd have a high chance of getting arrested, especially with my face.

"I don't trust that child. She's up to something. She keeps smiling at her sisters."

Well pardon me for being NICE to your brats.

"Right," says Mam. "I need to go to the toilet. Who wants to come with me?"

Deathly silence.

"Who's going with Dad?"

Eight arms shoot up. There's only four of us there. But we're making a point!

Four planes, 'tons' of fun and one café dinner later - I love café food. I love any food that Mam doesn't cook. We head for home. Mam counts us to make sure no one is missing, and Dad makes sure we've all got a share of the car rug. No one asks if "We're there yet" because we don't want to go home yet. There's something really magical about being out at night-time when you are a child. Mam tries to help Dad by being his co-driver.

"Did you see that sign? Watch out for that lorry. Brake for God's sake brake!"

Dad sings, *I Can't Stop Loving You* by Ray Charles. Anything is better than Englebert Crumpledick. Mam does 'tuts' in harmony and rolls her eyes. I start to feel tired and snuggle up to an already sleeping sister. A perfect day out.

As for proper holidays, well there weren't really many of them. We went to Sheffield with Nana sometimes to visit her family, but there wasn't any sea there, and it's not a proper holiday without sea. We went to Rhyl too. It seemed I just couldn't win at this holiday lark. Rhyl had sea, but no bloody sand! Was I jinxed or summat?

There was a time though when there was sea and sand and that's the time we went in care!

Oh yes, CARE!

("Don't you be telling people you went in 'care' young lady. They'll think you went in care!")

Me mam's talent for stating the 'bleedin' obvious' is at Genius level. Anyway, it turned out me mam was poorly with 'woman problems'. You have to say 'women's problems' half in a whisper and half silently. I just KNOW Les Dawson had stood behind her in the queue at the post office. When I first saw *Cissy and Ada*, I was gobsmacked.

"He's doing YOU Mam." (I didn't dare to say.) Uncanny resemblance. I came home from school one day, with the rest of the tribe. They loved our family at that school (we swelled the numbers ... stopped 'em from having to close down), and Mam was in the kitchen, as bloody usual. But with a STRANGER! No worries though, she was a lady. So that was alright. *Innit Myra?*

"How do you fancy going on a holiday?" said Mam. *Not bloody Rhyl I hope. What kind of beach has NO sand?*

"Where? Who with? Why?" (I was always a suspicious child.)

"This lady is a nun." (LIAR. She's wearing real clothes! Turned out she was one of them modern ones who went in disguise.) "And she's got a massive big house next to the sea." (There'd better be sand!)

"OK, when are we going?"

"NOW. I've packed some things for you all, and I'll see you in a couple of days."

"YOU'RE not coming?" (Was that a good or bad thing?)

"No luv. I've got something to do. Don't worry it's only for a couple of days."

"Is Dad coming?" (We'd never been ANYWHERE without at least one of them, or Nana and Grandad.)

"No. Dad's too busy trolloping about, and Grandad is poorly, so Nana has to look after him." Trolloping was Dad's job, Mam said. Must have been what they called lorry drivers, club promoters, crane drivers and singers in them days.

Well, this was going to be exciting. Off on our jollies without Mam or Dad. That meant I was IN CHARGE! I could hear the sound of six knees knocking behind me!

Now, it turns out, we weren't the ONLY kids she'd invited. When we got there, there were hundreds of 'em. I'd just seen *Chitty, Chitty, Bang, Bang* at the pictures. I knew a CHILD SNATCHER when I saw one.

We were shown to our room. I say 'our'. There were another 50 kids in there. Bloody 'eck, I thought our house was overcrowded.

I went into full defensive sister mode. I might be able to boss them about and cause untold misery, but NO other 'bugger' was doing it!

We stuck together like Siamese quadruplets for the entire stay ... TWO whole days.

It was OK, got to see real sand. But the food was worse than Mam's (to this day I can't eat non-Kellogg's Cornflakes).

It was great to come home (that feeling didn't last long), and for a few weeks at least, I avoided doing things that made my mam say "If you don't behave, you're going in a 'HOME'."

Never went to Rhyl again either. Every cloud and all that. And that's what Whitsun was. You got the pretty dresses and new shoes. That was the silver lining bit. But you couldn't have proper fun 'cos you weren't allowed to get dirty.

In fact, as a holiday, which in my book means fun, Whitsun was decidedly dodgy.

Look at Christmas ... The KING of holidays. Presents, great telly, lovely food (especially if Dad cooked) and chocolate for breakfast. Also the birth of the Baby Jesus (hurrah).

Easter. You didn't really get presents, not unless you count Beatrix Potter Egg Cups, and I don't! But you did get chocolate! Enough to almost make you wish you never had to eat chocolate again, emphasis on the 'almost'. The stomach of a '60s child was a wondrous thing. We were PRE 'E' numbers. It took a lot of fuel to make us hyper. Years later, two sips of 'mineral' and a purple tutti-frutti and my own kids were trying to abseil off the roof! But also Easter was about the death (so we thought!) of the once a baby, now a man, Jesus (boo).

Whitsun ... Well WHAT did Jesus do then? I decided to ask me mam. Wrong move!

"Mam. What's Whitsun?"

I see the 'fear' in her eyes. She's not sure! She's a Methodist. Their church isn't even a proper church. It's like a big shed, with chairs and, erm ... more chairs.

I'm a Catholic. We've got statues, smelly stuff, PEWS and Mary!

But back to my question. She's giving me the 'Look' (Why does this kid ask so many bloody questions?)

"It's something to do with Jesus walking somewhere."

"WHAT?" I always had a sarcastic lilt to my voice, which is why she probably responded to my query by giving me a clip round the ear. I'm told that at my birth, the midwife was quite offended when she first heard me cry.

So back to this 'Whitsun' thing, the only thing we got was new clothes. Clothes? That's what tight people gave you as prezzies, and I include me mam in this. Boosting up our Christmas present count with pyjamas and slippers and a dressing gown, all wrapped separately. Let me tell you, come Christmas morning 'soft' feeling prezzies were tossed aside. We all knew what was in them!

There we all were on Whitsun morning. New 'sailor' dresses ... again! I think me mam was born in the Canal ... she's got a proper thing about 'sailor suits'. Come on, Woman, the occasional 'sticky-out' dress wouldn't go amiss. But NO! Once you hit five she treated you like bloomin' Bobby Shaftoe.

New shoes too, and socks, knickers and vest. The lot! Hair brushed within an inch of its life and ten yards of ribbon. Maybe we could all plait the ribbons together, make a rope and escape. Just a thought!

And then comes the 'killer' line ...

"Right. Go outside and enjoy yourself, and get one speck of dirt, one teensy bit of tar on them clothes, and you're DEAD!"

Whitsun was CRAP, as was another special day in our house, shopping for clothes day. Now, younger readers might be confused as to why I'm including clothes shopping in a chapter dedicated to special occasions. That's because in the 1960s when your mam took you shopping for clothes, it was for one of two reasons and neither of them included the word 'fashion'. They were special occasions or school. You had no choice in what you wore. You just shut up and wore it.

"We're going shopping today."

"What for Mam?" I say suspiciously. Sweets is great, toys would be brilliant, but there's zero chance there unless Nana comes.

"Is Nana coming?"

"No!"

God, don't let it be ornaments. That blinkin' glass fish she bought last time is 'angin. I don't understand that woman. Won't buy so much as a pork chop but will spend a fortune on a pottery pig. Ornaments is me mam's 'drug of choice'. No window sill or empty space in the house is safe.

In the hardware shop:

"How much is that pot pig? Ten bob? Oh, very reasonable, I'll take it! It'll look lovely on my mantlepiece, will that. "

In the butchers:

"Two and six for a couple of chops?"(That Manc soprano of hers really makes me ears hurt!) "You must think folks are MADE of money. Give me ten pounds of 'stewing steak', here's the tuppence!"

"I'm making stew for tea 'r Lesley, and tomorrow we'll have 'hot-pot'" (Stew with pastry on top.) "And later in the week we'll have 'hash'." (Stew with extra potato.)

That pot pig is looking more appetising by the minute!

But back to our impending shopping trip.

"I'm gonna get you some new clothes and shoes." (OH MY GOD, it's worse than I thought.)

There is ONE bonus to being the eldest child. You get the new stuff. That's the good(ish) news.

The bad news is, where me mam goes shopping and her distorted view of how big I really am.

"The sleeves are too long, Mam."

"You'll grow into it." *Yeah, when I'm 25!*

"But I don't like it Mam. Can't we go to George Best's boutique?"

"Hark at 'er. Boutique? Remember lady, I don't get a 'penny' in family allowance for you and don't let your granddad hear you mentioning George Best. He's only just forgiven Bert Trautmann for being a German. No way am I turning up with you in any of George's stuff. We'll get disowned."

A true Blue was me granddad. I think he got it from me.

Years later, after Granddad had long passed, I caught her 'cheering' for Man United on 'Match of the Day'.

"What you doing Mam, have you gone colour blind? Them are 'reds'." (Shudder.)

"Well you might as well know, I've always liked them!!!"

Shortly after, there was a little earthquake in Manchester caused by me granddad turning in his grave. What a traitor! Who'd be such a disrespectful child! (Tongue in cheek, looking skyward.)

Anyway back to the glories of clothes shopping in C&A. Still it was better than Mavis' Modes on Moston Lane ... .all 'Crimplene' and old ladies buying pinnies.

One dress ("I don't care if everyone else wears mini's ... .and it'll be a mini when you grow into it") and a cardi later ... .and we're off to Clarke's for shoes.

Now SHOES were the one area where Mam would spend money, not on fashion, oh no! She went for COMFORT!

"If you're not on your back, you're on your feet. That's what I always say." *Liar! Nana said it first.* "So always invest in a good mattress and good shoes." (Good doesn't mean 'fashionable', FACT.)

How I dreamed of skipping round the streets in shiny white patent leather sandals with a heel! But in our house white shoes were only for Whitsun, even at my tender age. All hope was lost; I just KNEW I was coming out with FLAT black SENSIBLE ones. Maybe I could negotiate for ones with a buckle.

"How about these Modom? Just came in. Isn't the shiny buckle lovely?" *Hmm not bad.*

"NO, buckles break. Show me something with laces." (Sigh.)

"What size?"

"Thirteen, but bring me some ones and twos. She needs 'growing room'." *Me feet are gonna look like Coco the flippin' clown's.*

"Ooooh them are lovely." *No they're not, they're 'orrible.* "Let me just tighten up the laces so they fit better." (Ouch!) "That's it. I'll take 'em. Cheap at half the price, and 'r Melissa can have them next," (my face is like 'thunder') "and you can take that look off your face Madam, or I'll give you something to be miserable for."

I'm gonna be the laughingstock of Collyhurst. Cruel woman. I don't want good feet I want fashionable ones!

Years later when I got a job, I bought every pair of platform shoes and wedges Barratts had in stock. I've tripped over more pavements than a drunken soap star.

Nowadays I prefer flats! As me mam says "I'm not often wrong and I'm right again." She just loves being 'justified', and anyway most of me childhood photos are 'cut off' at the feet. Thank God for crap photography, little evidence remains 'cept for the mental scars. But what memories. And when I did get something I liked I wasn't about to share, as one or two of my sisters found out to their cost. In fact, there was only one member of the family who I would happily see in my best dress, and that was the Chosen One. My baby brother. Mam wasn't best pleased about that!

CHAPTER SIX
THE CHOSEN ONE (AND I DON'T MEAN JESUS OR JOSÉ)

"Mam, where's me cardi?"

"Which one?"

"The one Nana got me from C&A ... the pink one." *C'mon, Woman, how many cardis have I got?*

"Your sister borrowed it."

My eyes narrow. If I'd been white, I would have serious suspicions about me mam and Clint Eastwood.

"Which sister?" I ask nonchalantly, but inside I'm FUMING!

"Melissa." Sister number four. I think Mam overdid the Complan when she was pregnant, because for some reason Melissa has grown past numbers two and three and is nearly as big as me. She hovers round me like a vulture just waiting for the next outfit. There is an upside though. Sisters two and three have to make do with third hand stuff!

Mam continues, "Why don't you wear the white one I knitted?" (Cooking, sewing, knitting ... all things Mam is rubbish at!)

"I don't want to wear the white one, it doesn't go with my skirt," I lie. I'm calling for my friend Delia, and we're gonna try to get in the CIS building and ride the lift to the top. One hundred floors, I believe. I need to look half-decent. There's no way I'll get by the security guard in that hideous monstrosity, never mind that I'm only nine!

"Oooh! Get you, Twiggy." says me mam. "Well tough. You'll have to make do with what you've got."

(I think NOT!)

"So where's she gone?" I ask casually, hoping she can't hear the indignation and hatred in my voice.

"To the post office on Rochdale Road. With Jackie and her son." Jackie's

SON! He's riddled with impetigo. If she gets ONE drop of Gentian Violet on MY cardi, she's DEAD!

"Ok. Anyway, I'm gonna play out for a bit. See you later Mam."

I didn't even wait for any questions or permission. I bombed it.

So, what to do? I'm going to one end of Rochdale Road, and she is at the other. With MY cardi, and I NEED that cardi. For those of you unfamiliar with the local geography, imagine you are in Birmingham and you want to take a box to London. But that box is in GLASGOW.

Anyway, there was nowt else I could do, and luckily enough I didn't smoke then. So I went hell for leather and found myself outside the post office in five minutes flat.

I found her lurking by the bubble gum machine. Jackie was in the chemist next door but one, looking at 'rubbers' for her brat. *He's nearly three, why don't you just potty train him, you lazy cow?*

"Who said YOU could wear my cardi?" I sneered. She might be big, but I've still got five years and half an inch on her.

"I'm gonna tell Mam," she snivelled.

"Give me that cardi NOW, and if you go and say anything to Mam, I'll batter you AND never ever, ever, EVER be your friend again. No snuggles. No cuddles. Do you understand?" Her bottom lip starts to wobble. She idolises me. Am I being too cruel to my little sister? Nope!

One cardi later and I'm off to the CIS.

Nowadays, lifts and escalators are commonplace. Back then, they were the equivalent of a Blackpool fairground ride.

I met my mate and we bombed it down Rochdale Road. For once I was kid-free. Sometimes I think me mam had me for extra babysitting perks.

"Well now I've had Lesley, and I've got the help, why don't I have a million more? I'll just give her a couple of years to get some sense. Then I'll begin!"

When we first moved to Collyhurst, the CIS was the first thing I saw out of my bedroom window. I fell in love with it immediately, convinced it was the Empire State Building. Even though telly was in its infancy, its power was undeniable. I yearned for the day I could explore outside it. Maybe even find a bit of King Kong's fur. But that was before I discovered it had 'rides' aka the lift, and today our Mission Impossible *told ya telly was my life* is to get to the top. All 100 million floors. OK, twenty-five, but still, when the highest you have ever been is the second floor of a maisonette, well twenty-five is Everest!

We can see the tower of Strangeways too. Me mam says I'll end up there one day if I don't pack it in. Sounds good to me!

As I'm only nine, Mam doesn't really like me going to town without a grown up. But I've lied and told her we are just going to the park. What she doesn't know can't hurt me. *What she does know bloody does.*

"How many times have I told you? Don't do that!" Each word, and when she was really mad, each syllable, accompanied by a slap on the legs. *'60s parents took the job seriously.*

We are right outside the entrance now, trying to look casual. It's always good to whistle and look up in the air when you're trying to look casual. So why are one or two grown-ups looking at us suspiciously?

"Are you alright, chuck? Waiting for your dad?"

For a second I think we're outside Strangeways instead. "Er, yes and no!"

Nosy git.

"Are you lost? What you doing hanging round here?"

"We're waiting for her mam." I point to my friend who's a bit more goody two shoes than me and has been frozen into muteness ever since the nosy cow started interrogating us.

"OH! Is she the cleaning lady?"

WELL. I know we're not exactly the height of poshness but there's no need for that!

"No, actually she's a secretary who types letters and stuff."

Nosy git gives a little laugh. "OK, well see ya. Don't get up to any mischief."

As if!

She reaches the entrance, then turns back. *Bloomin eck, what now?*

"You see that man there?" *See him? Of course we can see him. The point is to not let him see us.* "He's the Concierge." *The WHAT? I thought he was the watchman.* "Tell him what floor your Mam works on and he'll let her know you are here."

God save me from interfering grown-ups.

"Fanks," *for nothing ... .now sod off!* "but her mam said just to wait." *The more you lie, the more you have to lie.*

"Hmmm". She mumbles and off she goes again. Thank God for that.

OK, time to get down to the serious business of actually getting past 'Hitler'. *I got that off my granddad. Anyone with a bit of authority is Hitler to him.*

"That bloody Hitler at the train station/on the bus/at Maine Road." Boy did the man get about.

We did have a plan, sort of. Most of my plans came from episodes of *Stingray*, and this one was no exception. So just imagine I'm Troy Tempest, *prefer being Marina but she wasn't in this episode* and me mate is 'Phones'. Well, the plan was that Phones would go up to the conci-whatsit and ask the way to Tib Street. *We knew where it was really, cunning!* I would then sneak past whilst he was busy, 'cos like me granddad said, "Give one of them buggers more than one thing to do and they're flummoxed." *Well, it began with F.* Me mate, being short, would then wait till two people were walking in at once and sneak in behind them. Couldn't fail!

Except it blinkin' did 'cos fairy elephant here got her cardi trapped in the revolving door. So instead of silently ensconcing myself in position by the lift, I merely wandered round and round in a panic trying to get me button out of the handle. He soon noticed me, and me mate didn't help by gawping and laughing.

"Ee-ar you two OPPIT before I give you a bloody good hiding!"

I should have just let me sister keep the soddin' cardi. Anyway, it was time to go home for tea. I was starving. I just hoped it wasn't stew!

I was lucky, though. Me mam's mate Jackie had been there all day, and she hadn't had time to cook. *God works in mysterious ways.* So we was having ham butties for tea. Hurrah! But that in itself presented another problem.

Why, oh why, is it so hard for mams to cut a butty into a triangle? I mean, it's not like they need a different knife or anything like that.

"You want TRIANGLES?" (Mancunian soprano's back!) "Where do you think you are, the Dorchester?" *If their kitchen's got hint of teak cupboard fronts, and a bright orange washing up bowl, then YES.* "I haven't got time to do triangles!" *No, but you've got time to smear gentian violet all over Jackie's son's head. I can see some still on your hand.* (I swear I'm adopted. I'm definitely Dad's. But you?)

"Anyway. Listen to this."

(She does that. Goes from one topic to the other without ANY warning.) Mrs Gartside, from Stovell Street, her daughter Susan died. *WHO? WHERE? WHO?*

"And me and Jackie ..." *Yeah Jackie, the one with a kid who has permanent impetigo, or as we called it 'The Mange', and thinks my dad "doesn't deserve you" simper, simper. The Cow! I'm not mithered at all what she has to say on the subject, she's hardly an example!*

I start flicking through my last week's edition of *Bunty* whilst I'm waiting for my butty. I'm so bored I start reading the Four Marys again. If I get any more bored I might even read the pony story. *Always gave the animal stories a miss. Don't get me wrong, I love animals. I'm just not interested in their lives.*

"...we were talking about how it must be the worst thing in the world to lose a child. BUT if it had to happen it would have to be one of you girls, 'cos when it comes to boys, I've only got 'r Wayne." I've definitely put down my *Bunty* now! !!!!! Oh yes! The 'Chosen One', 'r WAYNE. "I've got 5 girls and a SON!" That's how me mam describes her family, and let me tell you about him!

Nineteen-Sixty-Six turned out to be an eventful year for our family and the nation. You could tell something was brewing. Mam was getting 'fatter', and the midwife had come a few days earlier and left a massive box. I knew she was a midwife (whatever that was) because when she had knocked on the door, I had shouted through the letterbox.

"Who is it?"

"The midwife," she replied.

"MAM, it's the midwife!" I shouted to my mam, who was in the kitchen.

"Well let her in, you daft sod."

(You weren't saying that two minutes ago, when you thought it was the Clubman.)

The midwife stays for a bit, long enough for me to watch *Trumpton* in peace.

When she's gone I ask, "What's in the box, Mam?"

"Our new baby." *OUR? Speak for yourself, Woman. That bedroom's crowded out enough already with the four of us!*

Later on, I organise a meeting in my room, with my other sisters. (Alright, we got sent to bed, but it IS MY room 'cos I was there FIRST.)

"I know WHERE babies come from," I announce, enjoying the look on their faces!

"Go on then, where?" says number two. Number three is pretending not to be interested, *Snob!* and number four is trying to eat my face ... where is that kid's bottle?

"You see that box, behind the settee? It's in that!" I say smugly. "It's staying there for a bit. Then it's coming to live with us. Me mam told me."

"Well, it's not sharing my things," says number three. She still has 'Selfish Cow' syndrome from her days being spoilt rotten in Moston.

The next day, we beg and we plead. "Please Mam. Can we push the baby on the landing?"

"Go on then," she replies with a strange smile on her face. She plonks the box in the Silver Cross pram that lives in the hallway. We have a merry time up and down the landing with the 'baby'.

A few days later ...

Mam's still in bed. Nana's here, so no worries about dinner. Let her stay there!

The midwife turns up again. She goes in Mam's bedroom. I don't know what she's doing, but whatever it is, she must be rubbish at it, 'cos Mam's screaming her head off at her!

The midwife rushes out of the bedroom and grabs the box. *I don't think the baby can help ya, missus!*

We hear another scream. Then a cry.

"OK You can come in one at a time," says the midwife. "Eldest first." I smirk.

In me mam's room, the 'box' is open. Mam's still in bed, the lazy ...!

"Come here and see the new baby," she whispers. I give 'it' the once over.

"What do you think?" she asks.

"Nice," I reply. "What's for tea? And can Nana make it?" Afterwards, when we are tucked up in bed, we discuss the day's events.

"Innit horrible?" says number two. "What's that thing between its legs?"

"Dunno," says I. "We'll ask Nana tomorrow." It's been a long day, and we're all soon fast asleep.

Ah yes, 1966 was a glorious year. World Cup? What World Cup? That's the year 'r WAYNE was born. Mam's one and only SON! (Boy was he gonna get it!)

To be honest, after the fan-fare of his birth, we did our best to stay as far away from him as possible. Mam was always telling me I was a smart ars* girl, and I worked out all on me tod (gonna have to have a glossary in the back of this book if I want it to sell south of Wytheshawe!) that me mam (his too), had attached a 'bug' to him, which alerted her whenever one of us got within six feet of him.

"WHAT are you doing to MY SON?"

"NOWT! I'm just looking at him." (Mouth open, tongue covering lower lip. She can't see me, I'm not THAT brave.)

"And WHAT are you looking at him WITH?" He HAD to be 'bugged'. I had seen a similar storyline in *Stingray*. (Not the one I had adapted for the CIS visit.) Every time Marina was in a room alone with Troy (swoon), Atlanta turned up!

Now Troy Tempest is one thing. He saves the world. But what was so important about 'Wayne the Pain'?

"Oh yes. Doris, Edna, Norma" (or anyone who'd bloody listen,) "I've got a Son. That's right! A SON. OH yeah, and four girls too. But mainly a SON!"

As it turned out, he was a bit of a blessing in disguise. Mam was so busy pandering to his every whim, we got to do a lot more stuff behind her back, without getting caught out ... much!

And bless his little cotton socks. As soon as he could walk, he attached himself to me mam's skirt and hampered her every move for the next five years. Perfect, and a bit of company for Dad, too. He'd been out-numbered five to one before Wayne showed up. Not that it bothered Dad. He was always one for the ladies. I could tell you a tale or two, and I will in a minute. Go and get a brew, and let's have a gossip.

CHAPTER SEVEN
WHAT'S IN A NAME?

Have I mentioned my mam was an only child? Well, not technically. Granddad had been married before. He was widowed early on. His first wife died of consumption (TB), and they'd had a daughter who I will call Brenda, 'cos that was her name. Brenda was another one who wasn't 'best' pleased when me mam met me dad. Me mam, having quite an unforgiving nature when it came to her husband and kids, had sodded them all off so she didn't feature in our lives at all, which was just as good as being an only child to me mam, and us too. No aunts or uncles from her side. But so what! We had Nana and Granddad. Quality over quantity every time. With Dad coming from Barbados as well that meant actual blood relatives were thin on the ground during my childhood. My dad had his brother, who came to England with him, my lovely Uncle B. He lives in Flixton now, which is Mancunian for 'posh-ish', not quite Didsbury but getting there. A lovely man who contributed to my cousin list by at least six or seven. In fact, they are my only cousins over here, because even if the 'colour bar' hadn't affected my mam's relationship with her sister, it turned out that Brenda couldn't have children. God works in mysterious ways according to me mam. Hatred doesn't bring much happiness to those infected with it.

Dad's gone now. He died in 2008, but my uncle makes a nice substitute, and one day I'm going to sit down with him and pester him to tell me 'stories'.

Funnily enough though, although I've just told you about the scarcity of relatives, Dad did introduce me to a lot of 'aunties'! One day, not too long before he went to 'Work at Mays', Dad took me for a day out. "Don't you be taking my child in any trollop's house," were my mam's parting words, as we bombed it down the stairs. Dad taught me well. When Mam starts, you're not going to get a word in edgeways anyway. So might as well, get off quick!

My dad's Humber was parked outside the shops. There were some kids from Northern Drive sniffing around it with their mouths wide open. They'd called me a W*g a few days earlier, but I'd been on my own, so had to 'suck it up'. I wasn't chicken, but I wasn't stupid either.

They were getting a hefty dose of karma today.

That's right, you 'orrible little gits. Keep gawking! This w*g's got a CAR! I had the most triumphant smirk ever, as I slid into the front seat beside him.

YES, wishy-washy kids of today, WE could get in the front without being pinned in by giant reins. But having said that, a lot of us got killed in accidents. So WEAR a seatbelt please. Take off the please if you're reading this and you're related to me. Just soddin' do it or else. I'm more like my mam than I think.

A few years later Bruce Lee plagiarised that ENTIRE event for his movie, *Enter the Dragon*, replacing the racist kids with cops and changing the car to Jim Brown's passport. I never received a PENNY!

"Where ARE we going Daddy?"

"We gine guh see your Hanti." I'm just reminding you that he's Bajan, and I'm giving you something to aim for, in your head. I'll go back to Manc now! "But if your Mother asks, tell her we went to the Dogs at Bell Vue."

"OK" He didn't have to say another word. My loyalty to Dad knew NO bounds, nor no morality sometimes. My mam knows now that I'm sorry for some of the lies I told. I had to grow up and experience it myself to understand her. But back then I was a proper daddy's girl. He could do no wrong in my eyes.

We set off, and sometime later pulled up outside this posh house. Any house with a garden was posh when you lived in a flat. I found out years later we'd gone to Wythenshawe, so not so posh then. Dad got out and opened the door. "Come on, my Princess," he said, and whisked me into his arms, because he knew I was always a little bit shy when I went somewhere for the first time. I wrapped my arms tightly round his neck and we went inside.

I had a lovely day. There was a nice lady I called Aunty and a few kids. A couple of them were white and one or two looked strangely like me! We played out and did stuff, and Aunty did my hair in a new style. That one little thing would turn out to be the fatal flaw in our cunning deception.

Later that day, Dad brought me back home. He said, "Tell your Mother I'll be back later," and he drove off quickly!

She was in the kitchen. (Quelle surprise!)

"Dad said to tell ... "

"NEVER MIND what DAD said! WHERE have you been?"

(She was looking straight at my head.)

"We went to the Dogs at Bell Vue."

"And who did your hair? The Rabbit?"

(It's a hare actually, which is quite funny in the circumstances. Never mind.)

"Me dad!" (This is not going well!)

"Come here you, and remember what I told you happens to little girls who lie."

Apparently my nose will grow and leaves will sprout on the end of it. I'm almost willing to take the chance, just to see. But it's school tomorrow, and the other kids would take the mick.

"Ha, ha, ha, ha. You've been lying to your mam."

It took her fifteen minutes to get a reasonably believable story out of me.

"Get in your room and DON'T get undressed. We're going out later."

Oh God! She's putting me in a 'HOME'. She's warned me, now she's gonna do it. I know I'm always saying I can't wait to grow up. But I'm happy to stay here till I do!

I'm sitting in the bedroom on my own. The living room is next door. She's turned up the sound on the telly so I can hear that *White Horses* is on, hear being the operative word. That's just so cruel. I'm gonna tell Nana.

She sends my sister (number two) in with my tea. She's doing that sing-song voice thing "Yooo can't watch no telleeeee! ih, ih, ih, ih, ih!" I contemplate poking her eye out, with the nails on me French knitting bobbin. After all, in for a penny ...

It's dark outside now. Mam says "Right, you two. Coats on! We're going out for a bit."

Flippin' eck. It's gonna be an all-nighter at Jackie's house. We'll have to play with her scabby son. You know, the one with impetigo. He has purple blotches painted on his head. We'll have to sit there, bored to tears whilst they watch the soddin' *Forsyte Saga*, sip Cherry B's and plot my poor Daddy's death by land, sea and air. "I'll drown the b*****d. So help me, I'll bury him alive." You get the drift. But it turned out I was wrong. There was a taxi waiting outside for us, a big black taxi. (My God, she's won the pools!) It was a magical ride. Lots of twinkling lights in the night sky, beautiful.

We arrived at our destination.

We go through a door. My Uncle B is there. (How nice.)

"Oh, hi Joyce," he begins.

"Don't you Joyce me," Mam responds. (NOT nice).

"Is he in THERE?" she demands.

(Why even ask, you've barged past, before the poor man's had a chance to answer!)

He is in THERE ... sitting at a table with a LADY. He sees us, puts on his 'Black Clark Gable frankly-my-dear-I-don't-give-a-damn' face, and opens his arms for me and number two.

"Is that the LADY who did your hair?" says Mam.

"Err NO," says I, truthfully.

"Good God, man. How many have you got?" she says witheringly to Dad.

"Right luv," she says to the woman sitting with Dad. "Seeing as you like my husband so much, you can have his kids to match! Enjoy yourself. Oh! There's another one at me mam's. I'll drop her off tomorrow."

And with that she flounced out. Now that I look back, brilliant. Pure class.

We had a fantastic time, on our first ever visit to a nightclub! Coca-Cola in little bottles, with a STRAW! And when Dad sang with the band, we swayed at the side of the stage, like his mini backing group. He kept us there for ages, just to make Mam sweat; I overheard him say when he finally arrived back with two very sleepy but very happy children. I swear I could hear my mam crying behind the kitchen door. Dad had opened the door with his key; the only other person except for Nana who ever had a key to Mam's house. I don't think she had heard us come in.

"He's kidnapped my kids. He'd better get them back here right now or I'm calling the police!" A very illogical woman sometimes was Mam.

Speaking of relatives, she wasn't so keen on the Northern way of calling everyone Aunty or Uncle either. That comes from her tendency to be a bit 'snobbish', and we've teased her relentlessly but good humouredly, I hope, for years.

"Ay Mam. There's no way that John Sutcliffe can be the Yorkshire Ripper. He lives in a PRIVATE House."

But back to names. I can bloody waffle me, can't I?

A friend mentioned to me the other day, that when she was a child her brother conned her 'summat rotten' as we used to say then, by making her think her local shopkeeper, a lady with Parkinson's Disease, was called Mrs Nodder, and it reminded me of something.

I'm not putting down the 'youth' of today, but in my childhood you were raised to have manners. You wouldn't dream of calling a grown-up by their first name. Heaven soddin' forbid! It was Mrs So and So, or Mr. Whatsit. Unless, they'd been to me nana's for a 'cup of tea'. Then, they were 'Aunty Mary' and 'Uncle Eddie' and me mam hated that. To her, only proper family was family. Everyone else was a Stranger!

"Will you stop doing that Mam? They don't have any relatives round 'ere. You'll have them thinking half the bloody world is getting them a Christmas present. Our Lesley's already worked out she's got 29 aunties and uncles. She's expecting an Enid soddin' Blyton Christmas. God knows where I'm going to get 'lashings' of anything. She's a child proddy thingy, that one. I caught her reading the Cornflakes box the other day. Asked me what a 'Riboflavin' was. I didn't know where to put me face."

Oh yeah? But when me baby sister comes out with some 'goo-goo, ga-ga' nonsense, me mam's like, "Aw, int she clever, tryin' to talk." You can't win.

Anyway, back to my friend and Mrs Nodder. My friend had good manners, maybe in hindsight, a tad too polite. Virtually every sentence she spoke to Mrs Nodder ended with 'Thank you Mrs Nodder'. 'Can I get five Park Drive too, if you please, Mrs Nodder? Can you wrap the change in me mam's list, Mrs Nodder?'

"She's a weird woman, is that Mrs Nodder," said my friend, after one visit where ten items were requested individually, in her usual mannerly way.

"It's like 'good manners' make her mad. She was fuming by the time I asked for two ounces of cough candy."

Some names were well deserved, though. Me nana's friend 'Alice the Malice' so suited her moniker that you could almost imagine her mam saying "Think on 'r Ted. She'll have a nickname one day, and I can tell what it'll be, by the look on that face. Let's have one that rhymes."

My granddad had a friend called 'Fireman Bill from Rhyl'. Never been a fireman, didn't come from Rhyl!

'Dirty Gertie from number 30' was my nana's name of choice, for any woman who fitted her criteria for the title of 'tramp.' That's the woman type version. Not bearded man with knotted hanky version. Regardless of what number was on their front door.

My dad called me his 'long streak of misery'. In fact I was merely practising my poker/inscrutable ninja face for forthcoming confrontations with those whose motto is: "I brought you into this world, and I can take you out of it."

If you haven't guessed who I mean, you must be thick.

PS No disrespect to 'Thick' people (PC ... PC ... PC ... must be PC)!

Mam had a particular favourite name for me, seeing as she was convinced I could 'magically' make my face look the 'spit' of me dad's, just to spite her. You'd think she would have called me, Wonder Girl. Child of a thousand faces. But NO! She called me 'smartarse'. "Oy, little Miss Smartarse. Stop looking at me with your dad's face. But seeing as you are, tell me something? How come you know how far it is to the last inch from your dad's childhood home to the moon? But when I say don't go further than ten feet from the front door, you end up in Miles Platting?"

"'Cos I was thinking about stuff Mam, and me legs were moving at the same time, and when I looked up, I was outside Granelli's." *Has she fallen for it?*

"Well when a murderer gets ya I won't even bother calling the police 'cos I'll just think you're off somewhere THINKING. See how you feel then!" *Well I'll probably feel 'murdered' won't I?*

"Anyway Mam, I've decided to change my name. I want to be called Marina."

"MARINA? Where did you get that name from?" *Stingray!* If you came out of the kitchen once in a while, you might know what's going on in the world of telly and *Glamour*.

"And what's wrong with your God-given name, Lesley?"

"God didn't give it me. You and Dad did, and I don't like being called LES. "

Oh yes Mother, the girl who goes out with my friend Susan Parker's big brother. The one who's a hippie. She told me what it means ... ewww!

"Well you can call yourself Carmen Miranda for all I care. But when I shout 'Lesley', some kid strongly resembling you better get her backside in this house sharpish."

Years later when I married a Muslim, he suggested that I might want to change my name. He said it would make things easier, if we ever went to his parents' homeland. I wouldn't stick out too much as a 'foreigner'!

Well first of all mate, I'm English. We ain't 'foreigners'. Secondly, I'm not going anywhere that doesn't have a SPAR five minutes away.

But this name change thing sounds good.

"Hmm OK a new name. Sounds good to me. Is Marina a Muslim name?"

"Nope."

"Any names that sound like Marina?"

"Well. Let me think. There's Amina. It means ..."

"Sod what it means. I'll take it. Any chance you can change yours to 'Troy'?"

Way before all that, though, I was Lesley. Or Lesley Donna Maria Mottley when I was in serious trouble. I bet she really regretted giving all of us so many names. It wasn't a rare thing for ALL of us to be in serious trouble. It took an hour to get through the names. People must have thought there was a Girl Guide convention in our house.

Lots of sisters, lots of names, lots of kids. The only thing my mam had one of, was her single solitary remaining nerve, and we were getting on it!

Time for an escape or two.

CHAPTER EIGHT
GREAT ESCAPES

Much as I adore them now, in my childhood my siblings weren't exactly the loves of my life. In fact, they were sometimes a bloody hindrance. I spent much of my childhood trying to get away from them. Funny thing is, nowadays they are all my best friends and I couldn't imagine life without them. But back then ...

"Mam! Can I play out?"

"Who with?"

The Pope! Who do ya fink? "Me friends."

"Why don't you play with your sisters?"

'Cos I hate them. "Aw Mam, I don't wanna play with them."

"Do you know how lucky you are?" *Here we go again.* "I never had any brother and sisters, blah, blahdy blah."

I'm not surprised. Nana and Granddad must have took one look at you and thought, 'That's it, never a bloody gain.' Shame you weren't more like them.

"Where do you want to go anyway?"

There was a woman murdered on Rochdale Road, we're going to look for clues. "The Sand Park."

"You can go if you take one of your sisters."

Been here before, this is non-negotiable (sigh).

Right (tut). "Where's Karin?"

"No, take Tracey."

"AWW MAM! She's only two." *Look after your own flippin' kids.*

"No Tracey, NO Sand Park. Do I make myself clear?"

As mud! Ten minutes later, I'm ready for the off, baby in one hand, magnifying glass in the other. But first come the RULES:

"Have you got knickers on?"

(YOU dressed me!) "Yes."

"Don't talk to strangers."

What, stranger than you? "OK Mam."

"If you get lost, ask a lady to help you."

Yeah, I know a lovely woman, goes by the name of Myra. "OK, can I go now?"

"Stay within shouting distance."

Well I wasn't planning to go to the moon but ... "Yes Mam, can I go now?"

"OK But REMEMBER, I get to know EVERYTHING!" (The interrogation rooms at Guantanamo have a plaque dedicated to her.)

"Yesssssssssss! Can I go now?"

"Yes, but just nip to the shop for me first, and wipe that look off your face, or you'll be wearing it on the other side and I'll give you a slapped arse to match."

Down the stairs I go. There IS a rubbish chute, which you'd think would be quicker but when I pushed my sister Amanda down it she got stuck and the fire brigade ... anyway, that's another story (see Chapter 4).

Back I come, fags, cheese and a pound of stewing meat handed over. She counts the change. (This woman's got serious trust issues.)

"OK, off you go. I'll shout you for your tea. We're having stew!" *Oh God please let me be abducted!*

* * *

Mam never had any siblings. Her half-sister, B., was fifteen or so when she was born. So that doesn't count. Consequently, she had this romantic notion of us all being as happy as Larry (another random person we refer too without knowing who he actually is) and close. We were close alright. Put four kids in one bed and they can't be anything other than close, and damp too if one of them wets the bed. (Why's everyone looking at me?)

Mam's belief that we were the prototype for *The Waltons* and her deluded notion (although looking back, I totally agree,) that a big family was a happy family, were also part of the reason she wanted us to always be together. Paedophiles were another, but we didn't know that then. She would just tell us to "Always stay together and don't talk to any weird people," so getting to sleep out at someone's house, unless they were Nana and Granddad, was near impossible.

"What do you want to sleep out for? You've got all your sisters here!"

(Well there's a reason in itself!)

"Aw, but Mam?"

"No! I don't know who's in their house."

"Mam, you see Susan's mam every day at home-time."

"I don't mean that, I mean, well there might be 'funny' people there."

"Her granddad comes sometimes, and he takes his teeth out. But it isn't THAT funny!"

"I don't mean funny, I mean 'funny'. Oh never mind! NO! You can't sleep out."

"Well can I go to Longsight then, to watch them filming *Top of the Pops*? Jimmy Saville's gonna be there."

"NO!"

Cow!

And so it continued. Me asking, her refusing, until my soon-to-be 'best friend' moved to Collyhurst and a miracle occurred, and it wasn't even Christmas.

Delia and her family moved into Hewart Road flats, one floor up from me mam's hairdresser, the one who made her a foot taller every Friday. (Beehives could be scary!)

So one Friday (obviously) we're sitting there on the kerb outside the flats, waiting for Mam, popping tar bubbles and watching the comings and goings of Barbara the hairdresser's clientele. Some of them went in quite normal and came out with PURPLE hair!

Something's gone wrong there, I thought. I hope that doesn't happen to Mam. I'd be so 'shown up.' We were also watching the new people moving in. They had a MASSIVE telly (2" screen, 10' cabinet; this IS the '60s).

"Hiya," we say to a girl who looks about my age. (You don't realise until you grow up, how easily children make friends.) "Where have you come from?"

"Glasgow," she replied in a funny accent. Now I didn't know where Glasgow was, but I couldn't understand a word her mam and dad were saying. So I presumed it was somewhere foreign.

"You can come and play with us if you want."

"OK" And that was it. Best friends for life, or two years as it turned out, 'cos we moved. Even better, shock, horror, surprise! My mam LIKED her mam!

"Very nice lady that, got morals."

A few months later, I approached Mam.

"Can I sleep at Delia's tonight?"

"Yeah, go on then." I fainted. No, not really I'm just trying to convey my shock at her response. I was so excited. By this time the Glasgow accent was getting easier to understand. I think it helped that I was half-foreign myself! I could now understand almost half of what Delia's mam and dad said. We were going to have a great time, and Delia's mam could COOK! Ah, a proper dinner and I don't even have to wait for Dad to cook it.

We did have a fun evening. Such a nice family, and at bedtime, Delia's mam tucked us in. We told funny stories and giggled till we fell asleep. Well at least Delia did. Other people's houses have strange noises. I woke up in the night scared. I think I must have panicked a bit and started crying for my mam. After all, I wasn't used to sleeping out. But Delia's mam heard me. She sat me in the kitchen with her for a bit and made me some drinking chocolate. I didn't want anyone to know I was a 'scaredy-cat'.

"Dinnae worry," she said (I think). "It'll be our secret." And it was! Lovely woman.

It didn't happen too often though, the staying out thing. Not unless Mam was with us and that was usually because her and me dad had fallen out again. Let me rephrase that, SHE had fallen out with me dad. Oh I know she would have had her reasons, but I was a kid. A kid whose loyalty to her dad knew no bounds. So in my eyes it was always her fault. But the upside of all that adult angst was some great adventures.

"Come on you lot. Get your coats on, we're going round to Norah's." *It's the middle of the night, Woman. Well it's half past five, but it's nearly bonfire night so it's proper dark.*

"Can we watch the *Magic Roundabout* first?" I don't even really like it. But this is the '60s; only three channels. I'll take any kind of cartoon I can get.

"No." (Oh, but if it was *Coronation Street?*) "We need to get a move on, and hurry up. I don't want to miss the start of *Coronation Street.*" (See what I mean?)

Coats, hats, scarves and mittens (I can hardly move) and we're off.

"Keep hold of 'r Karin's hand. Watch Amanda on that kerb."

I'm not a travelling companion. I'm a bleedin' mobile Mary Poppins.

We arrive at Norah's flat. I'm quite happy really, I like coming here. Norah makes me mam laugh, and her kids are alright too. The eldest one, Malcolm Jr., (NEVER met Malcolm Sr.) has got a Junior Carpentry set. Our Wayne (The Chosen One) is too young for such wonders yet, and me mam is a proper sexist. So none of us is getting so much as a sniff at a 'boy's toy', not even a Lego brick.

"Happy birthday I got you a doll/book/French knitting set." *Yeah, thanks a lot.*

Anyway, me mam and Norah were soon settled in the kitchen (it's a woman thing). They'd got the Advocaat out, (looks like sick!), so we knew it was gonna be an 'all nighter'. It also meant that any man with any connection to either of them - in me mam's case: me dad; in Norah's: most of the regulars at The Dog and Duck - was in deep trouble! Mam had even brought her Englebert Crumpledick records and they'd dragged the Dansette into the Kitchen with them.

Leaving five kids in the living room, with a telly and tools. Well, what would YOU do?

The last time we had come to visit Norah (Mam found something in Dad's pocket), we had gotten into a discussion about the people in the telly. Malcolm Jr.'s sister, Yvette, (NOT Jr., her mam was called Norah, of course, and I'll tell you something else: her dad WASN'T called Malcolm either) - anyway, Yvette was of the opinion that everyone on telly lived in the back of it.

"So HOW come they are in my telly at the same time as YOURS?" *I'm surrounded by idiots.*

Now I know she was a full year older than me, but I wasn't stupid. I reckoned there was about Twenty-teen of them in each house's telly. BUT, they were all masters of disguise! If I'd known what MENSA was, I would have been firing off a postal membership form to them, right there and then. But we never had a stamp. Yet another obstacle to high achievement, placed in the path of the working class. Ta Granddad. You taught me well.

Anyway, I don't know about you, but I was raised to believe that God has a purpose for everything and I knew what the purpose of giving me access to a Junior Carpentry set was:

"Hand me that Hacksaw, Malcolm Jr., let's settle this once and for all. "

The plan was to carefully remove the back of the telly, say hello to the little people (I was dying to meet Troy Tempest), and put the 'back', er back. What could go wrong?

It's a good job Malcom Jr. already had an Afro, 'cos not only did people live in the back of the Telly, they had their own weather system. That bolt of lightning that hit Malcolm Jr. as he was trying to bend back one of the glass light bulbs to see if Skippy was in there, was a bloody big 'un. And by strange coincidence, all the lights in the house went out at exactly the same time. *Hurrah! That means candles. We loved it when me mam didn't have a shilling for the meter.* Funnily enough the landing lights went out too, and the street lights.

Mam and Norma thought it was a power cut and started moaning something about the 'bloomin' government'. It was so dark we all went to bed, and forgot about the telly, till the Wicked Witch of the West and Dirty Gertie woke us up in the morning, and they weren't best pleased!

We had no telly for a week. Malcolm Jr. and Yvette had NO telly! But at the end of the day, we still had a telly in OUR house and Christmas was coming up. That meant GREAT telly and its related problems, such as finding somewhere to sit when everybody was watching it at once.

CHAPTER NINE
TELLY

It's Christmas. Dad's home as usual. Never missed a Christmas did Dad - thank God, - he'll do the cooking. There's a James Bond film coming on the telly and we're all excited about watching it.

"Right you lot!" shouts Mam. "Come and sit down. The film's about to start." This is where the 'fun' begins. A mam, a dad, six kids and ONE three-piece suite. Now I don't know about you, but in our house, Dad got the big comfy chair nearest the fire. Mam got the other one. It's like the Three bloody Bears, and that left the settee between us lot.

"Mam, she keeps poking me."

"Well tell her to stop." Great parental skills.

"Mam, I think the baby's pooed. It stinks here."

"Right, 'r Lesley. Go and get me a nappy off the maiden."

WHAT! Leave my hard-fought-for comfortable position on the Settee? I'll never get it back. But if I refuse to go, well basically I'm buggered. Suddenly, a light bulb goes on in me head. I turn to my (very near) neighbour, sister number two.

"I've got to get the nappy for Mam," I hiss menacingly. "But I'll be back, and whilst I'm gone my shadow is minding my place." Bloody genius.

Number two looks at me with her trademark spiteful scowl. I have to be careful with this one. She's a little more savvy than the others and has even had the audacity to challenge my supremacy, once or twice. PLUS she's tiny and has a little curl right on the top of her head. So she gets away with MURDER!

"So you're telling me, madam, that our teeny-weeny cutesy little Karin, pushed that cat off the landing?" She really just said 'r Karin, but I'm trying to convey the attitude.

"Yes Mam, and I told her not to do it."

"Well, what was you doing letting her get so close to the ledge? Poor luv was probably trying to stroke it and it fell. It's not her fault." Good God, she's even immune to them eyes in the back of Mam's head.

But I digress again! Back to the seating arrangements. I've come back with the nappy. Mam's giving me a look as if to say "Where did you go for it, China?" The baby's laid on her knee all bare-bottomed and repulsive, (does she have to do that in here ... eww,) and there's 'Shirley Temple' sprawled out in my place.

I give her the 'Clint Eastwood'.

"Move out of my place."

"I didn't see YOUR purse coming out in Beddoes," pipes up the Mother.

"Aw but Mam, I TOLD her my shadow was minding my place."

"LOOK MAM!" shorta**e pipes up. "Her shadow's not even here."

"Sit on the floor 'r Lesley and SHUT UP. The film's about to start." Great film too. When I grow up I'm going to be a moggle first like Jean Shrimptom (I don't like Twiggy, too boney) then an actress and wear bikinis everywhere. I still want to be a nun though. I know, I'll be a nun who wears a bikini. That gold paint thing is interesting too. Mam's got half a tin of paint left over from painting the doorstep, and every other brick round the door frame. It's red but never mind. There's just about enough to cover sister number three. I know what we're doing on Boxing Day.

Fast forward to Easter. Same people present, same settee. Only difference is we're watching *King of Kings*.

"'r Lesley, can you get me ... ?" Yeah, yeah, yeah, it's always me!

I turn and face shorty. (She's not grown an inch since Christmas.)

"I'm going in the kitchen, and this time my INVISIBLE shadow is minding my place."

The look of defeat on the face of the 'enemy' is indeed a glorious thing, and what a brilliant idea. It became a family saying for the rest of our years living with Mam. We even devised a code for when outsiders were visiting. You know how it is, I'm sure all families have their own unique sayings, and it's tiresome and sometimes embarrassing having to explain them to strangers so if we had visitors we would just mumble at each other.

"My vis sha mind place." Clever clogs weren't we? But even better than watching telly with the mob was watching telly in 'secret' with just Mam. And what a crafty one she turned out to be. You see, when something special was on TV, but way past bedtime, Mam would sometimes say to me (after exaggeratedly looking around first to check we were alone and then continuing in her extra loud Mancunian whisper), "If you pretend to be asleep, when the others have dropped off, you can get up and watch *Miss World* with me." Oh my golly-gosh! Bedtime couldn't come quick enough, which wasn't unusual in our house. "It's SIX

O'CLOCK ... BEDTIME." Such a cruel woman. Having said that, being sent to bed and actually going to sleep, are two entirely different things. Six o'clock might be bedtime, but keep the noise down and you could have hours till actual sleep time.

So there we were, one bedroom, one bed and four kids. This was gonna require every ounce of 'kiss arse' I had accumulated throughout my short stay on this Earth, which ain't much. I have 'Eldest Child Syndrome'.

"I am soooooo tired," I said, adding a big yawn for effect, "I'm going to sleep." Three faces, similar but uglier than mine, turned round in unison giving me the one thing we ALL inherited from the mam. The Clint Eastwood narrow-eyed 'are you shitting me' look.

"I thought we was gonna play 'Magic Boomerang'," said sister number two. For the un-initiated, the Magic Boomerang was an Australian (who'd have thought!) TV series about kids who could make time stand still when they threw aforementioned boomerang. Earlier that day we had 'borrowed' the wooden boomerang shaped thing, off me baby brother's bunk bed. *Yes, he who has everything, the Chosen One. It couldn't fail!*

Flippin' eck! The ONE night I didn't want to make time stand still. Anyway, no point having a Magic Boomerang and NOT throwing it!

"Right," I said, in full big bossy sister mode. "We'll have one go, and if it works, we'll throw it over Mam and Dad tomorrow and sod off to Tib Street for a bit." Tib Street was Manchester's Disneyland. It had a pet shop and a joke shop - best bloomin' street in the whole of Manny.

We slid up the sash window, two kids each side; trust me it was hard work. Then we did that scissor, paper, stone game to see who went first. Number two won - the cow - and she threw.

I can report, it did NOT make time stand still. But it DID have the ability to make plant pots explode ... LOUDLY. Cue the entrance of Mam, stage right.

You can safely assume that Miss World 1968 went ahead with no involvement on my part. And I found out years later that I was not the only child she had encouraged in such deceptions. I was too young at the time to read the hidden meaning in sister number two asking me for the millionth time, "Are you asleep yet?"

See what I mean? Mam was proper crafty. But she was God-like in her absolute power. Just as she could give you telly, so, she could take it away.

"I see you've been in here for half an hour and still not tidied this pig sty. No telly."

"Who's put mashed potato in my plant pot? No telly."

"Have you moved that fireguard?"

"No. I've been sitting on the settee watching *Banana Splits*." (Not doing the sour grapes dance, which would mean moving the fireguard to have more room to move and also warm your bum at the same time.)

"Explain them corned beef legs then, and whilst you're thinking of a good lie, (how distrustful mother - I'm almost offended) you can turn that telly OFF."

"Aw, Mam. *Arabian Nights* is coming on next."

"*Arabian Nights* this!" *Ow! That hurt.* "You watch far too much telly anyway. Now go and tidy your room."

What does she mean, too much telly? I get up and help look after HER kids. Spend hours at school and all I want is a few minutes telly in peace on a Saturday morning. I'm running away, me, first opportunity I get. Gonna get a flat in Liverpool and be a Liver Bird. Too much telly? Is she mental?

How would she like it if someone told her to switch off the *Forsyte Saga*, or the *Onedin Line* or any of that other rubbish she watches. All boring old people, wearing clothes from the olden days and talking about feelings and stuff, and none of it in cartoons. When I grow up I think I'll get a job as the boss of telly. Then I'll make the news and news-like programmes (sometimes they fool you with titles, like *World in Action* - no soddin' action but loads of boring talking) suitable for both grown-ups and kids. If you're reading this post-1980, I hope you enjoyed Omnibus, the puppet version.

Loved my telly. It took me into a little fantasy world where posh frocks weren't just for special occasions, and I loved my posh frocks, especially sticky-out dresses.

.

CHAPTER TEN
STICKY-OUT DRESSES & OTHER DELIGHTS

One of my absolute favourite programs was *Come Dancing*. There was no 'Strictly' in its title then. I used to think the sticky-out dresses were beautiful, even better than the dancing, in all honesty. Some of them looked like proper tw**s. I'm a bit embarrassed to say it, but I also used to think the underskirts were one big mass of material, with holes cut in to put your legs through. I was a bright kid, but there were still areas of fog.

Sticky out dresses were my childhood love, after Troy Tempest and in later years Cliff Richard, I may as well own up. I'm bound to get 'outed'. Most of my gobby siblings are still local.

But sticky-out dresses ruled! I can vividly recall the day I was told by me mam that the sticky-out dress would no longer be a mainstay of my wardrobe. I was devastated.

"It's Whitsun next week. You're getting too big for a sticky-out dress now. I'm getting you something different." Too big? What about the bloody grown-ups who wore them? I tried to reason with Mam.

"They wear them on *Come Dancing* and they're all big."

"They're all prats too. Look at the fellas. How would you like it if your dad flounced around in skin tight purple crimplene?" She had a point!

But still, I felt so sad at the prospect of never having frills in my life again. I loved my sticky-out dresses. I would twirl around all day enchanting me mam with my presence, and a whirl of pale blue taffeta. She begged to differ though. What I called enchanting, she called "gettin' under my soddin' feet", and offered a choice of other activities and garments that she obviously approved of.

"Why don't you go and play by the railway line? It's a lovely day out and I can see you from the landing, so you'll be safe." In hindsight, really?

"Can I keep my dress on?"

"No. It might get caught in the track, and do you know what might happen then?" Her face had gotten closer and closer to mine with every word spoken. By the time she finished her question, her nose was almost touching mine.

"Erm." (Do NOT give a smartarse answer or you'll be going nowhere but bed.) "No."

"It might rip, and it cost me a bloody fortune. Now put your trews on and hurry up out. There's a train due in a few minutes. If you get close enough you can wave to the people. Just like the kids in that book."

The '60s were innocent times. Health and Safety wasn't even a twinkle in the corporation's eye. Turned out she was right not to let me wear the dress. Me legs would have got stung like mad with all them nettles on the climb up the embankment. And Mam never took her eyes off us (she'd made me take 'r Karin), or so she said.

It's funny 'n all how she said I would have to wear different clothes for Whitsun from now on, because every Whitsun after that I had to wear a bleedin' sailor suit of some sort. Navy blue at the top, white pleated skirt, or vice versa, sometimes as a dress. Black patent shoes, sometimes white, sometimes a sandal and a white plastic handbag. Just as an aside, have I ever told you the advice my nana once gave me in regard of handbags? Bear in mind I was about eight at the time.

"If you don't want to be mistaken for a prostitute, NEVER swing your handbag, especially in Piccadilly, and NEVER leave the price tag on your shoes." Sometimes it's good to take advice. If me nana was here now, she'd be proud as punch that never in my life has anyone mistaken me for a prostitute ... and that's all down to her. Ta Nana.

But back to the '60s. I've got a handbag I can't swing. Where's the fun in that? And it's Whitsun, too. The boringest of holidays 'cos you can't have fun.

"You get one speck of dirt or TAR on them clothes and I'll 'tar' your backside to bed as soon as you walk through the door. Now go outside and enjoy yourself. There's a Susan Hayward film I want to watch, and I want to watch it in peace." All said in her loving yet at the same time, threatening, Mancunian lilt.

Like I said tragic. But birthdays? Birthdays were brilliant.

For my ninth birthday, my nana and granddad gave me a ten shilling note. It lasted me for 33 years. That's about eight days in real money. Thinking back about it, am I sure it was my ninth birthday? Ten shillings was a LOT of money. It would have made more sense if it had been my tenth. Then I remembered. Granddad died three months before my 10th birthday. Maybe he knew?

Sorry, digressing again. So back to the ten shilling note. It was brownishy purple with swirls and a picture of the Queen. Or "that German living off my hard earned taxes" as me granddad called her. Granddad wasn't what you'd call a Royalist. But Nana, like me mam, loved them, never missed the chance to buy a commemorative tea cup, not that you could use it.

"Not that cup, you idiot. I'm saving it for 'best'." Confusing times!

If we'd have had Facebook back then, that ten bob note would have been my profile pic for weeks. That ten bob note took me to confectionary heaven. I could have bought at least ten boxes of Milk Tray. But I was a kid, quantity over quality every time. Me mam would always say, when one of us got some money, "Don't forget to share." Yeah right! It was YOUR choice to have so many sprogs, you feed 'em.

I could have filled the bath with the amount of Spanish gold and mojos I got through, and I did share. I gave all my sisters a white chocolate mouse EACH. I hated white chocolate and having to share unless it was someone else's stuff. Not selfish. Normal. We didn't get much, and it was not bloody fair having to share when you did get something. But we always did, 'cos me mam forced us to.

I won't lie, we were poor. I didn't realise it at the time, although me mam's constant refrains of "I'm not made of money" and "NO! you can't have it" should have given me a clue, but in my childlike mind I just saw it as Mam being Mam, a miserable mean cow!

But we got by, and on birthdays we always got money in a card from Nana and Granddad.

"Yeah, lovely book Mam. I'm gonna enjoy reading *Cinderella* AGAIN! Where's me card off Nana and Granddad?"

"You love money too much, you do Madam. Here you go. Mind how you open it. You're not a pig!"

I swear she makes up random sayings as a hobby. Learn to knit like other mams. Last time I looked, Pinky and Perky weren't exactly overloaded with envelope opening duties. This is exciting, it feels like a big one-half a bloomin' crown. I'm rich beyond my wildest dreams. I'm sure Nana and Granddad can't be related to me mam. She doesn't do NOWT for me. I'm not talking about food or clothes or stuff like that. That's her job!

"Why don't you save some for a 'rainy day'?" (*We live in Manchester, it's p*****g it down. That day has come Mother.*) "Anyway it's Sunday. You'll have to wait till the shops open tomorrow."

WAIT! With half a crown burning a hole in me hand? Is she mental? I'm a Manc, luv, where's there's a will there's a wake. I'm off to Granelli's first soddin' chance I get. Granelli's is the ONLY shop within a hundred mile radius open on a Sunday. I'm telling you mister and missus, the '60s were hard. Come Christmas, if you hadn't got your fags, beer and bread in by Christmas Eve, you were going without till January, and every Sunday was like a mini-Christmas 'cept no presents and definitely no turkey. You had a roast chicken though, which unlike nowadays, always tasted of chicken, and not a shop open for miles. I miss that these days.

I eat my 'Birthday Breakfast' crispy bacon, fried eggs (soft but not 'snotty') and 'bakes' (Bajan pancakes); luverly. I have to admit Mam does lovely birthday breakfasts. After breakfast I open the rest of my prezzies. It's tradition in our house for everyone to get together and watch the present getter open their presents. Which is OK as long as you don't catch your sister's eye when you open one from one of Nana's friend, 'cos they'll try and make you laugh and then you get done for being an 'ungrateful sod'.

"Oh, barley sugars ... how nice."

Dad's got me Cinderella high heels, pink see-through plastic with glitter in. I'm gonna 'clip-clop' up and down that landing till the neighbours invent ASBO's.

It's the Summer Holidays, which has its good points and bad points when it comes to birthdays. I was born in August - it's usually sunny - but I never get to take sweets in for the class. I bet me mam had me then deliberately, the tight git! Once the presents are all opened, I'm itching to get off and spend some of this money. Sunday or no bloody Sunday.

"Can I play out now Mam?"

"Where?"

"Oh, just on the railway lines at the back." *It was all good clean fun in the '60s.*

"Go on then, and don't lose that money, and take a ..."

"Yeah yeah, I know. Take a sister. C'mon 'r Karin."

Actually, I don't mind the company (for once!). Granelli's is in Miles Platting and some of the kids there are rough. It's good to have the back up. Our Karin's a shorta**e but she can proper scrap.

We get there unscathed. It's not as good as a proper shop, but I get some bits and bobs and discover 'Fisherman's Friends' are 'angin.' Like I said, limited choice. But a girl's just got to spend, spend, spend.

Later that day I get an overwhelming urge for crisps and nuts. I know! The 'offy' at the side of the 'Sparrow' pub will be open soon, and KIDS can go in that bit!

Me and 'r kid loiter outside watching people come and go. I don't know what goes on in there. Some of 'em go in normalish and come out all wobbly and talking funny.

"All reet petal" (see what I mean) "where are you two exotic beauties from?"

"The flats up the road." (Nosey git)

"No luv. Where you from originally?"

"Er ... Moston!"

"You don't get a tan like that in Moston. "

(Ha, ha, ha, not heard that one before.)

"I get it from me dad. He's a heavyweight boxer and a cowboy and he's got a gun. He's a bit mental, really. Any more questions mate? Oh I've got one. Where do YOU live?"

"Cheeky Bugger." (You're getting off pretty sharpish though.) We hear the bolt going on the offy door, hurrah.

"Can I have six bags of crisps please? Three cheese and onion and three smoky bacon. Four bags of nuts ... and, erm ... I'll take one of them plastic combs. "

"It's not a comb, luv, it's a cond ... oh, never mind."

"OK ... I'll have a bottle of Dandelion and Burdock instead, then. "

Me and my sis are stuffed. I'm a good sister. I share with her, 'cos she stood by me. But them lot sat on their nappy-clad backsides all day. They're getting nowt! We settle down on the settee like the bezzy mates we are (at least till the sweets are done). The look on the others' faces is priceless. If they behave I might let them lick the empty bags.

Next day Mam says, "Why don't you go to the paper shop and treat yourself?"

I've only got thruppence left. Why oh why couldn't I wait? It's me sister's fault, she always leads me astray. I'm gonna batter her and that copy of *Twinkle* she's hiding behind ain't gonna help her. Wait a minute. That's not *Twinkle* she's reading. It's MY *Bunty*. She is DEAD!

CHAPTER ELEVEN
NOSEY-PARKER

My mam likes to tell the story of how I could read before I could walk. She says the reason for my serious face on all my baby pics is because I've read the photographer's reviews.

"Why smile? It's gonna be a s**t picture." But that aside, it's true, at least I can't remember not being able to read. It had its ups and downs though. When me mam was in one of her 'moods', a gift often given to her by Dad, it was like reading was some kind of offence.

"Sit UP at the table young lady. What ARE you doing hunched up like that, anyway?"

"I'm reading the cornflake box."

"Reading the cornflake box?" Said in her Mancunian Soprano - luckily we couldn't afford crystal. "Haven't you got anything better to do?"

"I'm learning stuff," said with my 'I am surely adopted' voice.

"Well learn your backside out of this kitchen. Who's ever heard of a kid stuck in the house like you?" *She was to live and learn, when she saw her great-grandkids surgically attached to Playstations*. "Get outside and get some fresh air. And take a sister."

Outside it was. But I sneaked a comic out with me and sat on the stairs between our floor and the one below. The stone steps were cold on my bum, but at least I got a bit of peace and an hour or two uninterrupted reading - except when people had the cheek to want me to move so they could pass.

I read anything I could get my hands on. I remember reading in my nana's *Tit-Bits*, a magazine. Not in front of her. Mam thought it was a bit rude. Kind of like a seven-year-old reading the *Daily Star* nowadays. She'd popped to the shops for some fags; the doctor had just been. I know it seems like I'm making it up, after all who has a doctor come to their house these days, except maybe the doctor's wife, but I'm not lying. They actually came to your house when I was a kid. How weird is that? The doctor had told her to cut down from her Senior Service. So, she'd be 'dilly-dallying' for ages in the shop trying to choose between Woodbines and Park Drive. I knew me fags me, both Mam and Nana smoked like troopers. Dad had his special cigs (nudge, nudge, wink, wink, marijuana), and Granddad had a pipe. When me mam gave up smoking in 1970, I realised it wasn't a cloud of depression that seemed to follow me, whenever she was around. Cigs and smoking were something everyone did, and I was used to it. Came in very handy too, did all that smoke. With Mam and Nana's cigs and Granddad's pipe all going at once, sometimes, if you stood very still, they couldn't even see you were there. Good news for a nosy kid like me.

But like I was saying about the *Tit-Bits,* there was this article about how a woman on the 'pull' could show she was 'willing for NOT a shilling' (I swear it said that!) by putting two melons on top of her trolley in the supermarket.

Now, what was meant by 'pull' was a mystery to me, and where melons came in to it, I just didn't know (not till I was somewhat older). But I did know it was 'rude,' and 'rude' was funny!

Take for instance the wonderful moment that was the delivery of Mam's new catalogue.

When you heard the knock on the door and saw that massive book outside the front door, it was a cause of celebration ... eventually. Because no one, not a solitary single human being or kid, was allowed to look at it before Her Majesty. She was the same with the TV and *Radio Times.*

"YES! You can look at it. But NOT before me, and BEFORE I look at it I'm going to bath the baby and wash the pots and clean up the mess YOU made, and put you'se all to bed. Then I'm gonna sit down with a cup of tea and a fag and read it very, very, slowly. I suggest you ask me again in two days' time." (What a Hitler ... relatively speaking.)

But eventually, just like the *Radio Times*, the catalogue was ours. We huddled together, delightedly poring over pictures of toys we would never have. For example:

The Cadbury Miniatures Machine

Any form of Meccano

Legos ("You'll lose them.")

Design your own fashion wheel *What kind of rubbish is that?*

Yes, Mother, it still hurts. I could have been the next Coco Chanel (next Coco the Clown me mam would have probably said).

Anyway, after we'd had a quick look at the toys and skipped passed Kitchenware and Bedding (boring) we came upon ... UNDERWEAR! Our favourite bit. This required a plan. Fortunately we'd just watched *The Great Escape*, and discovered another of me mam's ' I can't stand its' (she had loads of them).

"Will you shut up with that damn whistling. I can't stand it." (Well sit then!) "And it's unlucky for a woman to whistle in the house."

(I'm not a woman I'm a girl.) "Why is it unlucky?"

"'Cos it IS ... ..Now SHUT IT!" (The standard Mancunian Mam code for "I haven't got a clue but I'm bigger than you so there!")

Time to put that plan into action. "OK troops let's do this." Sister number three stands guard at the door. It's her job to listen out for movement in the vicinity of the kitchen. Sister number four is positioned at the front window. Not for any particular reason. We live on the second floor, it's not like anyone is likely to walk past unless the circus is in town and the man on stilts has got family round here. But it gives her something to do and makes her feel included.

Me and number two hold our breath for a few seconds. Mam can appear from nowhere. She's like a pantomime baddy. All of a sudden she's behind you! When we're confident the 'coast is clear' we slowly turn the page, and there they are in all their glory. Bras and men wearing knickers. How funny is that? Even funnier than Abbot and Costello, and THEY are funny. Some of the models have long knickers, like what Nana wears. We can hardly control ourselves. Tears of laughter stream down our faces. But there's a sad side too. Some of them are obviously suffering from disfigurements. Some of them swellings are hideous, and why do the women have a beard in their knickers? When I look back I suppose that was my first introduction to porn! Ewwww! Rude stuff was funny for a bit, but no substitute for the innocence of our childhood television programmes. In modern times there seems to be less and less distinction between adult stuff and child stuff. I consider myself very lucky to have been raised in such innocent times, when anything on telly before 6 pm was totally suitable for the kids. One of our favourites was *Captain Pugwash*. My bestest character was Master Bates. But a couple of my sisters preferred Seaman Staines.

I preferred books and magazines to telly though. You could learn so much from a magazine, and get the most amazing bargains too. Now what Northerner doesn't love a bargain, especially that other great reader in the family, Nana? Not books, though. In between 'doing' for half the women in the posh houses near the Bluebell Pub, and sorting out the doctor's surgery and the Ben Brierley, she didn't have time to sit down with a good book, so she stuck with her beloved magazines. I tried to get her interested in my Enid Blyton collection, but she declined.

"You're alright, chuck," she had said, after I tried to interest her in the plot for *The Wishing Tree*. "I don't read for the stories, I read for the adverts." Now me nana was as down to earth and sensible as they come. But when it came to anything with 'Miracle' in its title she was a con man's dream customer.

"Nip to the post office, 'r Lesley, and get me a five bob postal order. The *Tit-Bits* has got a great offer on The Miracle Fatbuster."

Ooh! Where's me duffle? "Can I have a sherbet dip?"

"You can have a million sherbet do dahs when I win the pools. Me Lucky Leprechaun number predictor out of *The News of the World* arrived this morning. Viv Nicholson's gonna be coming to us for a borrow."

"Yeah, right. But can I just have ONE sherbet dip whilst I'm waiting?"

I got the postal order and the sherbet dip (happy days). Nana let me put the letter in the letter box too, very exciting for a '60s child. Five days later, it arrived, a big lump of plastic. Me and Nana thought it was great. Mam just sat there with her 'withering' look.

"Mam, when will you realise these adverts are just a con?"

"Listen, Miss Fancy Manners. I'm sat here today because of my Fatima holy water necklace. You've always said that was a con, too. I would have died in childbirth with you if it hadn't been for that necklace."

"Mam! You left it in the doctor's when you went for your checkup. It's just a coincidence that your 'waters' broke when you went back for it, and let's have it right. You only live two doors down from the surgery."

"Are you saying there's nowt peculiar about my 'waters' going, exactly as I stepped foot over the door? As I live and breathe - just! What happened ay? I ended up having a blood transistorradionation (her word, not mine!) That's what. If I'd been at home in me kitchen, I'd be standing here dead now. You'd have killed me!"

She's from Sheffield. They talk a bit like us. But they've got funny 'ways'.

Anyway, never mind that. That's a classic trait in our family, we're great at talking to, yet still ignoring each other, in this family.

"Look at me underarms now, and again in ... erm. Ooh! INSTANT RESULTS it says on the box. Hold this cardi." I like Nana's arms just the way they are. All soft and wobbly, perfect for cuddles. It looks like one of them hairbrushes you get, in a dressing table set, the ones with no handle. The ones I have no idea 'what to do with'. Me mam says it's to brush your clothes. Yeah right, like me clothes have a beehive! Underneath it's got loads of little wheels all going in different directions. It's beige plastic with a darker beige trim. It kind of reminds me of a model caravan.

Nana reads the instructions for how to 'instantly and miraculously dissolve unsightly arm wobble and discard those chiffon sleeves forever'. Seems simple enough. Wow! She's really giving it some 'jip'. She doesn't move this fast when she's showing us how to do the *Charleston*.

"Right 'r Lesley. Do me arms look different to you?"

Think I'll go with a lie but only 'cos I love her and don't want to hurt her feelings, or let Mam think she's right. "YEAH Nana. It's magic."

"Oh shurrup you idiot," says me mam. To ME! If it was nowadays, I'd need counselling for emotional abuse. But it's the '60s, this is normality.

People can laugh all they want at my nana, but it's thanks to her that we got to have a colour telly. The 'transform your black and white telly to colour INSTANTLY' ... erm ... transformer, arrived last week. Only 5 'n 6 plus postage - a BARGAIN! It's a big sheet of coloured see-through plastic. The top is blue, for the sky. The bottom is green for the grass, and the middle is pink, for the people. This was before mass immigration, so you 'ave to allow it! It's a bit of a bugger when *The Black and White Minstrel Show* is on. Mam thinks it's horrible and demeaning, but Nana lets me watch it. I don't feel one bit 'demeaned'.

I had to look that word up in me junior dictionary. The next time Mam offered me 'stew' for tea, I replied, "No thank you Mam. I find it very demeaning to eat stew."

I spent the rest of that day trying to find a comfortable position to sit in. She only went and smacked me with the 'buckle end'. Bloomin' eck! You can't win in this house. They teach you a word and you get done for using it!

Anyway, I reckon my nana has saved my life many times with her wonderful knowledge of superstitions. Because of her, and Granddad too, I have never put new shoes on a table, opened an umbrella indoors, although I have poked number three with one many times. I've stepped into a dual carriageway rather than walk under a ladder. I cross everything I can when a hearse passes me, inhabited or not. I throw salt over me left shoulder and greet magpies like they're family. I rub me Buddha on me lucky leprechaun then stick me lottery ticket under them, and to this day, touch wood, nothing really 'bad' has ever happened to me. I've never won anything either, but it's just a matter of time, innit Nana? I've just had a thought. Maybe I'm cancelling out me leprechaun luck by squashing him with me Buddha?

I wish Nana was still here, not least because if Mam was fuming about something, she was the one who could calm her down and make her see sense, and that was a lot, because Mam was constantly fuming.

CHAPTER TWELVE
WE'VE MADE HER MAD. NOW LET'S MAKE HER A PREZZIE

The only thing programmes like *Blue Peter* did, in my humble opinion, was to highlight social inequality. I didn't know a single solitary human being kid, who's mam EVER had a spare piece of sticky back plastic lying around. Anytime my mam got a piece of Fablon, it went straight on a cupboard door front, and as for empty washing up bottles, they went straight from kitchen sink to bin!

"I'm not having any rubbish left lying about in this house." *Well, get rid of the other 59 kids you have running all over the place then.*

"Anyway, what do you need a bottle of washing up liquid for?"

"I don't need the liquid, I just need the bottle. There's only a little bit left. Can't you put it in one of the baby's bottles?"

"You still haven't answered my question. WHAT DO YOU WANT IT FOR?"

I'm not bloomin deaf. "I want to make a model of Thunderbird 1."

"And what's that when it's at home?" *If you weren't permanently attached to the kitchen you'd know.* "Mam, It's only the best programme on telly." Except maybe *Stingray.* I'm torn.

"You mean it's a rocket? But you're a girl." *And?* "Go and read a book or something, and listen to me. When girls do boy things, it can affect them in later life. I can't say much 'cos you're too young to understand. But believe you me, you do not want to be wearing checked shirts and upper lip hair when you're older."

"I don't get it Mam. What do you mean?" I wasn't lying either. What was this mad woman going on about?

"Where's me old movie news annual? That's the one. Now look at this. The men are called actors and they do man stuff, like this picture of Rock Hudson looking under the lid of a car. See. He's doing man stuff. The ladies are called actresses and they wear pretty dresses and do lady stuff, like all these ladies behind him. Building a rocket is man stuff. That's why men like Rock Hudson do it. If the ladies started doing it, Rock Hudson wouldn't like them."

Hmmm. I don't realise at the time, but I'm storing this conversation in my memory bank. In years to come me and Mam will be discussing this again, once she gets over the shock!

So, I never got my empty washing up liquid bottle. But one day, me and *Blue Peter* had a cosmic coming together. They had a 'to do' that I could 'DO' - a no-bake cake.

Also, by amazing coincidence, it was just before Mother's Day. You can keep your bubble bath in a diddy bottle, Woolworths. My mam's a Queen and she's getting a cake fit for a Queen.

Well, that was the plan!

I gathered the others in the bedroom, which was getting more crowded by the day. Will she ever stop this 'baby' thing?

"Right, you lot. We're making Mam a cake for Mother's Day."

"We're not allowed to touch the cooker," piped up number three. Little Miss Follow Rules.

"SHUT UP, Lady Fauntleroy! I've got it covered. It's a no-bake cake, and it's called a crinoline lady cake." The others seemed suitably impressed. I told them about *Blue Peter* and how easy it was for Val Singleton to make. We took a vote, four to one in favour of doing it. But wait, there's four of us in here, so where did the opposing hand come from? For gawd's sake, 'r 'manda does that Tippy Tumbles have-to-go-everywhere with you. I thought something was funny when I was doing the vote count. I can't recall any of us being white before, nor that plastic-looking.

Once we sorted that little mix-up out, it was time to sort out the ingredients. It was easy. All we needed was:

Chocolate: We could pool our 'spends' to get enough and sister number two was short enough to sneak in the kitchen unnoticed and nick a couple of Penguins if we didn't have enough.

Rice Crispies: Hmm bit of a problem there. The Mother only ever bought cornflakes. Still, we could crush 'em up. She'd never know the difference; got no sense of taste anyway. Couldn't have had, not with her stew.

A round bowl for the shape of the dress: Next door's dog has one and it's always left on the landing. No harm in 'borrowing' it for a bit. Sorted!

Icing: The amount of iced fingers me and Nana got through, we were bloody experts at making icing. But then again, how hard was mixing sugar and water?

Icing bag: Who's that 'posh' round here? We usually slop it on with a spoon. I know. We'll use one of Mam's rubber gloves! Perfect.

Sweets to decorate: Valerie Singleton used silver beads, but you can only get them in town and anyway, they're expensive. We're gonna use them sweety necklace things. Number four can bite them off for us. She's too young to be much use in any other department.

A Doll: For the actual 'lady' part of the cake. You didn't eat that bit, just in case any idiot, or sister number three are reading this. The doll part was a bit of a problem. This was not long after my foray into the world of 'hairdressing', and all the dolls in the house looked like extras from *Dawn of the Zombies*. We certainly couldn't afford to buy one; pinching one off some other kid wasn't an option either. Talk about serving up the evidence to Judge Dredd on a plate!

"Where did you get that doll?"

"I found it." (Innocent look, eyes raised skywards, fingers crossed.)

"I swear, you'll end up in prison, you." *Great, you can come and visit me and Dad at the same time. Save on bus fare.*

Suddenly, number two came up with an idea.

"Why don't we use me mam's doll?"

"She doesn't have a doll, you moron. She's a grown-up"

"Yes she does." (I'm getting me mad up, now.)

"NO. She does not! I'm gonna batter you in a minute."

"Yes she does." She holds my gaze, but she's moved to the other side of the room, just to be on the safe side. "It's in the toilet covering the extra toilet roll." Maybe we are related after all. The kid's a genius!

So, there we were, ingredients all sorted. We were well on our way to making the best present Mam had ever had. Just one more teeny problem, hot water. Easy solution to that one.

"Mam, I've got tummy ache."

"Aw, do you want me to fill the hot water bottle?"

"Yes, please." Kerching!

It's Saturday afternoon. Nana's here. She's watching wrestling and pretending to listen to me mam moaning about MY dad. Never mind Dad, I'll marry you when I grow up, and I won't NAG.

"So I said to him Mam, 'What do you take me for?' blahdy blahdy blah."

"Yes, Luv, he's a cheeky sod. C'MON MCMANUS, KILL THE BUGGER!"

Genetically, I'm doomed, but the both of them are preoccupied as usual. We won't be missed for an hour or so.

"OK ... are we ready?"

Hot water into number four's potty. Chocolate broken into pieces and put in dog's bowl. Bowl placed on potty. Somehow, I'm not tempted to pinch a piece. This part took ages but eventually we got there.

Crush up cornflakes. Number four can stand on 'em the fat cow.

Cornflakes in bowl, leave to set. No fridge, but no central heating either. It's bloody freezing on that window sill. It's gone rock hard in no time. OH SUGAR! We forgot to put the doll in before it set. Never mind, I'll gouge a hole out with me compass. Not the getting you somewhere one, the sharp maths one. *Aren't there enough words in the English language so they can have one each, Mrs Queen, or whoever invented it?*

It's not a full doll anyway. The bottom half is material, which covers the toilet roll. We can stuff that down the hole easily. It's looking good-ish, and the dog is gonna get a proper treat with all the chocolate still stuck to his bowl. Better than Pedigree chum any day.

Icing mixed. Hole bit out of rubber glove. Now for the Fanny Craddock technical bit. Bloomin' eck, that Val Singleton wants a slap, this ain't as easy as it looks. We don't have the luxury of access to 'one we made earlier' unlike some. Miss 'I'm so posh I've got two ovens' Singleton. But we got there in the end. The dog or number four can lick up the mess. Bits of the sweet necklace now, as a finishing touch. I'm sure that kid ate more than she bit off.

LOOKS PERFECT.

I spend the next few hours trying to get me mam to force it out of me.

"We've got you a Mother's Day present Mam. But I'm not telling you what it is. Do you want to know what it is?"

"No thanks, luv, I like surprises."

I bet she thinks it's bubble bath.

"It's not bubble bath. Do you want a clue?"

"No thank you, I'll wait till tomorrow."

"Should I give you a hint?"

"NO THANK YOU I'LL WAIT!"

Ungrateful ... person.

Six o'clock the next morning we all rush into her bedroom. We have no problem getting up early on a weekend, but Monday to Friday?

"Aw that's ... (long pause). That is lovely. I'll eat it later."

"NO!" Six voices in unison. We sound like a choir. "Eat some now!"

"OK Hmm, lovely. How did you make it?"

I give my Clint Eastwood 'look' to the others. "It's a secret recipe Mam."

That was many moons ago. But Mam, if you're still interested in how we made it, the recipe is above.

That wasn't the only gift we made or bought for Mam. We were such perfect and thankful children and really, really kind too. It's a pity she was so ungrateful. I remember another time ...

Me and some friends were playing in an old mill one day. Couldn't tell you where, but we crossed over Rochdale Road, near my school, St. James, just outside me dad's office, 'something' Bookmakers it was called. We were careful to avoid the cars that sped by every HOUR, traffic was so much lighter then. Then we jumped over the River Irk, and ran up the sandhill. You had to do it fast, or you just came tumbling down again. Actually, I preferred to walk up a bit and climb the bit of the hill that had grass you could hold on to; not 'chicken', practical. I did run up the sandhill once. Did it in record time, so I'm told. It was the day a bloody great big rat came sauntering out of the tunnel, like he owned the place. I say 'HE', I didn't stop long enough to find out, which upset sister number two. She was addicted to *Animal Magic* on the telly.

"Ooh! was it a boy rat or a girl rat?" How I longed to be just like me mam - an only child!

Eventually we got to the top of the hill - many routes, one destination - and ahead of us stood T'MILL. Smashed windows, collapsed floors, dangling wires - DISNEYLAND.

It's a shame all those derelict mills were pulled down. Poor kids nowadays have got to make do with 'Fun Factories' full of SOFT PLASTIC BALLS. Where's the fun in that? We had wrought iron ones.

It's nearly bonfire night. So that means it will be Mam's birthday soon. Twenty-one again! Money is a bit tight, as I'm sure it was for all nine year olds round our way. I remember her 21st the year before.

"What do you want for your birthday, Mam?"

"Oh, don't bother with all that nonsense. It's just another day to me."

Two days later, we overhear her chatting to a friend, "The kids never got me a THING! Not even a CARD!"

Back in the mill. We turn a corner (carefully) on the second floor. There in front of me lies the biggest cotton reel you've ever seen. You could French knit a Scarf for King Kong with that. It's beautiful, Mam will love it. She can put it in the living room and display her collection of women in 'sticky-out' dresses. They look like dolls, but they smash. (Oops!)

We roll it back up to Rochdale Road. That took some doing, all the way up Collyhurst Street and onto Thornton Street North. We avoided cutting through the 'Flats' in case any bigger kids robbed us. Then up TWO flights of stairs and banged on the door. I never had a key, and so desperately wanted to be a 'latchkey kid' like some of my mates. But SHE was clever. She worked NIGHTS. "What do you want a key for? I'm ALWAYS here when you come home."

She opened it, took one look at us standing there and declared, "If you think you're bringing that piece of rubbish in MY house, you've got another think coming, and why are you hanging about with HER?" She means Susan Long. She's twelve and the one who asked me to go to the mill in the first place. "Sod off you, and don't take my daughter to places like that again, or me and your mam will be having words." God, I feel so shown up. Susan will never speak to me again. Me mam is so UNGRATEFUL. All I wanted to do was give her a prezzie. Now she's made me mate fall out with me, and she won't stop moaning about it.

"What made you think I'd want that piece of rubbish in me house, and let me catch you playing in them mills again and there'll be trouble, Madam. Do I make myself clear? You could die in one of them places, and trust me, there'll be murder round here if I catch you going round with them bigger kids again. They encourage you, and you're an idiot. Do you want to die?" Well that's a stupid question. Of course I don't. Why is she so obsessed with death?

CHAPTER THIRTEEN
MURDER AND THE MANCUNIAN MAM

In 1971 we moved to Langley, which was not unlike Collyhurst, just with houses and a bit more grass. I think Mam would have stayed there forever if we hadn't gone to Barbados for a few years. But anyway, it was nice. If I'm really honest though, to me it wasn't proper Manchester. But hey, I was just a kid, and kids had no say in anything.

One day me mam and me nana were sitting in the kitchen; it's a compulsory thing for the women of this family. The only reason no one sat in the kitchen at me nana's house was it was the size of a cupboard. But the kitchen at Langley was massive, and there was a hatch between the kitchen and the living room, which was a deal-maker for me mam and I thought it was good at first, too. I remember thinking I can just ask Mam to pass me a butty through the hatch. I need never miss an episode of *The Tomorrow People* again. It went both ways did that theory, according to me mam.

"I'm in the kitchen, but I'm keeping the hatch open. That way I can see everything you lot are doing." *Bloody great.*

One day, Nana came for a visit. I was getting older, then, and a bit too cool to be getting excited by her visit. I answered the door, not even looking up from my copy of *Jackie* (*Bunty* was for babies).

"Oh hiya, Nana. Mam's in her office."

"Cheeky Madam. Don't be rude about your mam, she can't help the way she is." I looked up and Nana winked at me. Sod being cool - I loved that woman.

"Be a luv and put the kettle on. You make a nicer brew than your mam, but don't tell her I said that." I laughed.

I put the kettle on whilst Mam showed Nana her latest ornament purchase.

"It's lovely, pet. I've stopped buying ornaments meself. It's this new decimal money. It confuses me. It's one thing saying something only costs ten pence but that's two shilling in real money. So how much did that giant brandy glass cost? FIFTY PENCE? That's ten shilling. You could buy a house for that when I was a girl!

It's like a Monty Python sketch is going on in the living room, only no one's laughing.

"Tea's ready!" I shout, and sit down to read. The hatch is open, so I can hear every word they say. I read and they prattle on about everything from Nana's veins to my dad's latest trollop.

"Well, don't say I didn't warn you, Joyce. Don't get me wrong. I've got a lot of time for Callie, but he's always had an eye for the ladies. He married you, though. Don't you ever forget that. Enough of them tarts have passed through his hands and his whojamaflip, in the last few years, but not a one have made him want to take that ring off your finger. "

"Mam! Do you have to be so crude? Anyway, this house is in my name so he can stay with whichever tart he wants to."

"Do you two MIND. That's my dad you're talking about. Really!"

"Oooh hark at her! This is what I have to put up with day after day, Mam. Lesley and her one-woman fan club. "

And this is what I HAVE to put up with. The wanton destruction of my dad's reputation. Don't get me wrong, I knew he had his faults. I just chose to ignore them and blame Mam for everything. I was hell as a teenager.

At least they have the grace to shut up. I carry on reading my *Jackie* and it goes quiet in the kitchen for a while.

Then I hear Nana say,

"Does it not make you think 'r Joyce," *so THAT'S where she gets it from*, "that her name's a Jinx?" *Whose name? And what's a 'JINX'?!*

"Well, I'm keeping an eye on her mam. The kids are NEVER out of my sight." That's a lie for a start. Go in the garden, Woman. The others escaped through that gap in the privets ages ago. They're all hanging round Middleton Arndale as we speak.

"Well mind you do, 'cos think on! There was that Lesley" (*my name, why are they saying MY name*) "Ann Downey. Then Lesley Whittle and now poor Lesley Molseed."

What ARE they going on about?

"I know, Mam. It's doesn't bear thinking about. She's an idiot and she thinks the sun shines out of her dad's a**e, but I wouldn't be without her for the world." *Gee thanks. I watch a lot of American stuff and I'm picking up the twang.*

I do a bit of investigating by reading through some back copies of the

News of the World when Mam's in the bath. I'm not allowed to read it, but just happen to be passing the top of the airing cupboard where she stashes them and can't help myself. I found out these poor girls who shared my name had been tragically killed, and for a short time, thanks to Burke and Hare, sat there in the kitchen and my own vivid imagination. I thought death was waiting for me round every corner. My best friend at the time was called Lesley, too. When I told her about it, we spent a few weeks s******g ourselves.

* * *

Funny though, how death and murder played such a big part in my life, it's a miracle I'm still here today. Not a week went by when I was a kid that didn't involve risk of death, mainly at the hands of me mam.

Take for instance, something as simple as a day out with me mates.

On most Saturdays I could either go to the 'baths' OR the 'pictures'. Not both, like everybody else in the world's kids. "I'm not made of money! Who do you think I am, the Queen of the Bank of England?"

"There's no such person."

"Are you calling me a LIAR? Do you want a good hiding, young lady?" *Yes! And no!*

So one thing it is then. Which to choose? Baths? Great fun. Pictures? Great fun. In the end the 'baths' usually won. My logic being that seeing as we had a telly, I was pretty much guaranteed a film now and then. Whereas I could only do a stroke and a half in our bath and there was usually a sister taking up the tap end, which reduced it to a single stroke. Rubbish, when you believe you're Miranda the Mermaid.

The other thing that swung it for the baths was the drink machine.

I know better now, but in them days, you ask any kid where they want their food coming from and trust me, machines won over mams every time. Bloody eck, I couldn't wait for the day Sunday roast was a pill like on *Lost in Space*. Or, even more true to life in my opinion, U.F. blinkin' O. Bring it on, 1980. But, back to this, drink machine. It served tea and coffee (for old people), but we were there for the BOVRIL. I can't remember how much Mam used to give me. I had enough to get there on the bus, enough to get in and enough to get the bus home OR get a Bovril. Are you starting to understand how deprived my childhood was now? Tough choice, and added to that was Mam's warning: "Don't ever, ever walk home, it's too far. You could get killed, and if I ever find out you've walked home I'll kill you." So there I was, Bovril in hand, stranded in Harpurhey. I wasn't on my own. Sister number two had come with me, and not by invitation either, plus two of our friends. They all went for the drink/walk option, too. Me friends had Bovril, but me sister being a smarta**e decided she wanted a hot chocolate. Due to her excitement at having a button to push, she pressed the wrong numbers and ended up with coffee. Black, no sugar, extra strong. How I laughed.

OK, better start walking. We knew it was a straight run on the bus because we didn't have to grip the seats like Billy Eck (who, actually, is he?) to stop from falling onto the floor, as it rounded the corner. It also had no doors. *Health and Safety, Madam? P**S OFF.* And, we could see the CIS building, our homing device, nearly all the way there. If only we'd thought on, THAT was from the TOP of the bus. Street level was an entirely different thing. We asked someone (a lady) the way.

"Oh, straight on luv till you come to the park, and then left onto Queens Road and you're home."

What could possibly go wrong? The PARK, that's what. What harm could it do to have a few goes on the swings. After all, was it our fault that the actual proper park bit, swings, roundabout, etc., was right there in full view of the main road? Obviously meant to entice children, of which I was one! We had a great time, till some bugger nicked the sun. We bombed it home.

Mam was waiting, and me friends' mams were there too, and a POLICEMAN! *What's this, a party?*

"I'll KILL YOU," she screamed. "I thought you was dead!"

Strange woman!

Then there was the time I decided to stay behind after school and help 'Miss' change the picture wall.

"You're a good help, young lady. I'm glad your mam said it was OK for you to stay behind. We'll get this finished in no time."

Sugar! I forgot to tell her. She won't miss me. She's got loads of other kids there. She won't even notice I'm not there. Keep saying that girl, you might even start believing it.

"Where the soddin' hell have you been? Your sisters had to walk home from school ALONE. 'r Karin was a nervous wreck when she got in. "*Nervous wreck? Half the street is frightened of that evil midget you call a child. She was probably shaking with temper 'cos some poor sod got away.*

"I was helping Miss at school. We ..."

"Helping Miss? Helping Miss?" *I'm not deaf, no need to repeat yourself.*

"I thought you was DEAD!"

Bloomin' eck. Talk about worst case scenario. What a pessimist.

"I wish I was dead! I hate it here. I get the blame for everything!" See? I told you I was advanced for my age, not even a teenager yet and having moods already.

"Oh, sick of it in here are you?" She's taking it literally now. I didn't mean IN here. This is the living room. The only room with a telly.

"Well you can go in the bedroom then. Now sod off or you're dead!" If I'm out she worries that I'm dead, and if I'm in she's threatening to kill me. I can't win.

CHAPTER FOURTEEN
PETS TO POORLINESS

We couldn't have big pets when we moved to Collyhurst. Mam said it wasn't fair with us living in a flat. I begged to differ, behind her back.

We'd grown up with pets living at Nana and Granddad's. There was Roger the dog. Roger was a girl, by the way! A beautiful Collie. I nearly fainted the first time I saw *Lassie*. How the flip did 'r Roger get in the telly? A conundrum that baffled me until some months later (see Chapter 8) and Joey the kangaroo! Only kidding. Joey was a budgie. Nana, to our great delight and Mam's mortification, had taught him to say "Sod off you cheeky bugger," and "I could 'murder' a cuppa". Now there's a funny thing, the amount of death threats associated with food and drink in our house.

"I could murder a cuppa."

"I nearly caught my death going to the shops in this weather."

"No. I haven't murdered Thumper, eat the soddin' pie. Bloody Walt Disney."

"I swear to God, if I come back in this kitchen and there's any tomatoes left on that plate I'm going to prison for murder!"

"If you swallow that chewing gum, you're gonna die."

"Too many sweets make your teeth fall out. Then you can't eat anything at all ... and you die!"

"If you touch my Milk Tray bar, you're DEAD!"

But back to Joey and Roger, I loved the night-time routine we did with them. Don't tell me mam, but on Saturday nights Nana and Granddad let me stay up dead *that word again* late. It was so late there wasn't even any telly on. The middle of the night, practically. Eleven o'clock! About half an hour before, Nana would get Joey ready, and let me tell you something, Joey was thick. He fell for the same trick every single night. Me nana would go up to him with a piece of cloth hidden behind her back.

"Who's a cheeky boy then ... is 'r joey a cheeky boy?"

"Sod off you cheeky bugger ... God save the Queen."

"Bloody Hell, Flo," piped up me granddad one night. "What did you teach him to say that rubbish for?"

The Queen was a bone of contention between them two. Granddad was a socialist, someone who shakes their stick at the telly whenever they see the Queen or Harold Macmillan.

"They want to try working down the pit for a day, and then try telling us 'we've never had it so good'."

"You've never worked down a pit 'r Bob. You're a wages clerk, and the Queen never said no such thing. I think she's lovely."

"Well, I'm only standing up to go to me bed. Not for that bloody anthem, and my father worked down a pit, so think on, Flo. I know what I'm talking about."

"Shut up, you miserable git. I'm sorting the bird out."

That was as bad as it ever got when Nana and Granddad argued.

"Right. Night, night, Joey. "And then, all of a sudden, she'd throw the cloth over the cage. Within seconds Joey was fast asleep. Worked a treat on a bird. Not so great on a sister.

"Mam, 'r Lesley keeps throwing her coat on me."

Then it was time for Roger. As soon as Granddad started poking the fire out, Roger would turn round three times and settle himself on the hearth. I loved that dog.

Dogs and budgies however, meant fur and feathers. Nana didn't mind, but Mam did.

"It's bad enough having to clean up after you lot every day. I'm not cleaning up after a soddin' dog."

"I'll do it, Mam."

"YOU? Who can't walk from the living room to the front door without leaving a trail of disaster? I don't think so." Charming.

Mam just wanted the house all hoity-toity and doilied up, and this was in the days when kids couldn't hold mams and dads to ransom. So I tried negotiating.

"Can I have a cat then?"

"No."

"A rabbit?"

"Only for tea." Ew! You Wicked Witch of the West.

"A hamster?"

"What part of 'no' do you not understand? N. O. bloody NO, and if you don't stop that skriking, I'll give you something to skrike about!"

By this time my pleading was accompanied by wails and sobs. I knew her threat was a real one and worked hard to stifle my crocodile tears. *Well, you didn't think I was that mard did you?* I just didn't do it quickly enough. She did that all the time. Set false time limits.

"I'll give you thirty seconds to shut up."

Five seconds later:

"Right. That's it. BED!"

I sat in bed, sobbing genuinely now, and looking forward to the day I left home. Being seven, that was a little way away. But hey, never mind, and in the meantime, there was always another option.

A pet she wouldn't even know I had. A caterpillar. They were lovely. All colourful and fluffy and sticky. They turned into butterflies too. What a bargain for a Northern lass. Nowt gets wasted. That was the motto in our house.

I'd been to Queens Park a few days earlier and there were loads of them, free too. The value of this pet was increasing all the time. Mam didn't exactly like them though.

"What's that crawling in your hair?" I was hoping it was nits. She'd keep me off school because of the shame, and I'd get to watch *Trumpton*.

"Oh my God, it's a caterpillar. I bloody hate creepy crawlies!"

It WAS a caterpillar, Mother. Whacking it out of my head with the baby's bottle, and doing a war dance on it in your stilettos has killed it, and I've got a lump in me head now. Perhaps I can still get that day off ... concussion?

But getting a day off school was even more difficult than trying to get a pet. If you wanted one, my mam had the following requirements:

A Death Certificate or,

Photographic evidence that hell had frozen over.

It was also dependent on what day of the week it was. Saturday or Sunday, no problem. Monday to Friday? Not a chance. Unless ...

"Mam," (whingy voice) "I'm not well."

"You don't look not well to me."

What kind of English does she speak?

"But my tummy hurts."

And I haven't done me homework!

"That's 'cos you won't eat sprouts."

WHAT?

"Have you been to the toilet?"

"Yeah."

She's so embarrassing.

"Come ere ... stick out your tongue. Let me feel your head."

She watches too much Dr. Kildare.

"Hmm your head does feel a bit hot."

It will do. I've been resting it on the 'immersion' for the last half hour, and this was the days before 'Lagging'.

"Right then, back to bed, and remember! Poorly kids DON'T watch telly, or play with toys. When I come back from taking the other kids to school, I'll give you some syrup of figs." Wow, thank you. I can't wait. "I'll tell Uncle John next door to listen out for you till I get back."

He's not me uncle, and he's called Tom! Lovely man, though. Used to tell me stories about the old days and gave me tripe with vinegar. I was certainly a strange child, I loved tripe, but then again, anything was better than me mam's stew.

Oh my God, ALONE in the house. I reckoned I had about thirty minutes to do some serious 'rooting' - more if she saw someone she knew and started gossiping about some poor sod's dirty nets. Why doesn't she be 'Christian', knock on the door and offer to boil them. If she's not boiling 'stew' she's boiling nappies. Gets her money's worth from that pan, does Mam.

I didn't dare to go in her and Dad's room. She booby traps it. "Who's been in MY room? I stuck a hair across the door and it's gone."

Are you a mother or an MI5 agent? What the heck have you got in there?

I've opened every cupboard and drawer in the kitchen within seconds. There's a big bag of nut brittle. I open it up, there's a note inside: 'I've counted the pieces.' Bet you haven't measured them though. I break a piece off and pop it in my mouth. Me 1, Mam Nil.

A quick slug of the baby's Delrosa, eww, sickly! A bit of Gripe Water (lovely), and it's time to position myself for her return.

How should I lie? Literally not verbally; I'm already a master of that. I lay flat on my back and cross my arms over my chest. Blinkin' eck I look dead. I shift about trying to see if I look 'ill' enough in the wardrobe mirror. I wish we had a rubber hot water bottle. I need to maintain my 'high' temperature and this stone one is a bugger to position on your head.

I hear her outside.

"Was she any trouble, John?"

"No, chuck, and it's TOM. "

"Aw, thanks. I'm making some stew, should I send a bowl over for you?"

"No thanks, luv, I'm going out." He's housebound! Smart man is Tom. My mam's stew is 'anging. But for anyone interested (and slightly disturbed) here's the recipe:

MAM'S STEW

Good for torturing young children and making dads take over kitchen duties.

INGREDIENTS

1 to 7 lbs. of stewing meat *dependent on amount of sprogs at any given time*. Also please note, no particular animal or meat type is mentioned. This is not a typo. Unnamed meat is cheaper.

A 'nunion'. Well that's how we say it. Water, lots. Potatoes, lovely as chips, 'orrible in stew.

Salt and pepper to taste, if she remembers. Carrots for colour, but mainly 'cos we hate them.

Seasonal veg also make this a very versatile dish. For example, add sprouts and you have festive stew.

An OXO cube, if there's any left. If not, chuck in some gravy browning.

INSTRUCTIONS:

Take one large pan; the one for boiling nappies is ideal. Remove nappies first ... Or don't. It makes no difference to the taste.

Peel anything with a skin, leave fat on the meat; it's good for kids. Anything that looks and tastes horrible is good for kids.

Chop up anything little mouths can choke on. Some of you may have a kid with a big gob. Leave an extra big piece of fatty meat, just for her.

Put the peeled and chopped stuff in the pan. Fill to the top with water. Boil for hours. Serve.

Leave kids in kitchen with threat of 'death' if they don't eat every last bit.

Watch *Forsyte Saga* in peace.

Re-enter kitchen. Smile at empty plates. Send kids to bed.

Feel suspicious. Borrow next door's dog to sniff out food left behind immersion heater, in plant pot on window sill and wedged beneath mangle.

Find additional chunks in Ewbank

Visit kids' bedroom, take belt, use belt.

Clean kitchen. Go to bed.

Get up. Serve leftover stew for brunch. Yes, we do 'posh' on weekends and school holidays. Stay in kitchen whilst every soddin' last drop of 'brunch' is eaten.

Thank God I was 'poorly,' and even if I wasn't, just the thought of that stew made me queasy.

The bedroom door slams open. If you've ever seen that bit in *Misery* where Kathy Bates is miffed with James Caan, you'll know what I mean.

"Right! What's wrong with you?"

I start coughing. "I just feel proper poorly Mam. "

"Can you feel your toes?"

What am I supposed to say to that?

"Er, a bit."

"Hmm, you've got the 'Mange'. I'll get the syrup of figs." *Jesus, Mary and*

Joseph!

"Ee arr, get that down." I swear she's getting some kind of perverse enjoyment from this.

"Don't gag. I'll tell you now, Madam. I don't care how long it takes, you're having every last drop on that spoon."

I am so telling my dad about how she treats me when I'm (supposedly) poorly.

She's tucked me in so tightly I'm gonna need Harry Houdini's help to get up.

"Right. Stay there, and don't move. Do you want some stew?" *God, NO!* "No thanks, Mam. But what if I need the toilet?"

"Shout me."

"What if I feel sicker?"

"SHOUT ME!"

"What if ..."

"Just BLOODY SHOUT ME!"

No need to get 'nowty'.

The day drags. I look around my bedroom. No telly, no radio, no nowt. Kids nowadays don't know they're born. After what seems like an eternity, my sisters come home.

"School was great," says number two.

"We had a surprise visit from Ali Bongo off the telly. He came in at 'assembly time' and did some tricks and stayed till home time, visiting all the classes."

I start to feel genuinely ill. I think I'd just experienced my first bout of karma! It didn't matter what I tried to get. Whether it be a pet or a day off school, the end result was always the same. Bed.

In fact, every day ended up with me being sent to bed, and she didn't need much of an excuse to bring bedtime forward, either.

I'll tell you in a minute about the time she sent me to bed, because of my FACE.

CHAPTER FIFTEEN
WHY'S YOUR FACE LIKE THAT?

Tell me something, why do mams have kids with dads whose faces they 'can't stand'? Even as a child I understood basic genetics. Kids look like their parents. Why me mam seemed constantly surprised and annoyed by this was beyond me. 'Oooh let me have kids with a man I'm going to hate so I can constantly be reminded of his presence, and let me do it six times!'

"I can't stand him Jackie. His lying cheating face knocks me sick, and them kids better stay out of my way today, 'cos if a single soddin' one of 'em comes in here looking at me with that 'look' they got off him, there's gonna be murder." I think I'd better get myself a balaclava.

"You're too good for him, Joyce. I wouldn't have given him half the chances you have. It's them foreign ways. Don't you wish you'd married that lovely lad Lawrence now?"

I just happen to be passing time, on the landing outside our house. The kitchen window is open, so I can hear every word being said. That Jackie is a proper cheeky mare. *Mind your own business, you ugly cow. My dad wouldn't touch you with a bargepole, and who the flip is Lawrence? I'm telling me dad.* Turned out Lawrence was some lad me mam used to 'court' in the olden days. She kicked him to the kerb when she met Dad. Can't knock her taste, but that Jackie has got to go.

I hated them kind of mates me mam had. Sitting in our kitchen calling me dad. And the cheek of it too, coming from someone who's one and only kid was top to toe impetigo. Never seen Jackie's 'husband', either, but by the look of the kid I reckon he came from the land of purple people.

I was almost tempted to shout something cheeky through the window. But that would have been disastrous on two levels. First, I would have given my presence away, and second, me mam would have battered me for giving cheek. Never mind, I'll have to settle for throwing dirty looks when she gets up to go. Or maybe I could leave one of me roller skates at the top of the landing steps. On second thoughts that's too obvious. I go inside and walk into the kitchen.

"Mam, can I have a banana?"

"Go on then. Take it outside though. It's too nice to be stuck in the house, and me and Jackie are having a chat." *I bloody know you are, you pair of character assassins.* "And make sure you put the peel in the chute. Don't want anyone to slip on it. They'd break their neck."

"Of course, Mam." Not my fault if it falls out of the chute, is it?

"What you up to anyway?" I can't tell her I'm plotting to break her mate's legs, so I lie.

"Now't, I'm just gonna sit on the landing steps, eat my banana and read a book. I wanna wait till Dad comes home. I need to tell him something."

I shoot Jackie a dirty look. *Yes you tramp, I'm gonna tell him about you.* Mam shoots me a dirty look back, the type that says 'Don't you dare show me up.'

I hang about at the end of the landing. I can hear them going on. I hate people like Jackie. Just 'cos she's got no husband she thinks me mam shouldn't have one either. Suddenly, I have a thought. *It's my house, too. Why should I sit outside?* I summon up every ounce of brazenness and breeze into the kitchen, copy of *Bunty* in hand, and plonk myself down at the table.

"It's cold outside, Mam. Can I have a cup of tea and some biscuits?" I shiver, for effect. Mam gets all concerned, she's good like that.

"Let me feel your hands. Oooh, you're freezing. I'll put the kettle on." She and Jackie try to continue their conversation. But because me and me little ears are there, they have to leave out words and conversation becomes almost impossible.

"So I said to ---------- you piece of ---------- I'm ---------- cabbage. "

"Don't blame you. The ----------. You should have ---------- cakehole!"

Mam gives a sigh and ruffles my head. "We'll talk later, Jacks."

'Cos she's standing behind me, she doesn't see the look I give Jackie. Imagine your worst enemy is in church with you. They are sitting on one side of the church all on their own, and you are sitting on the other side with the rest of the congregation and the choir. It's dead quiet. Everyone's just finished singing *All Things Bright and Beautiful*, and they're waiting silently for the priest to give his sermon. When all of a sudden your enemy trumps. Well, my face was a combination of that and Clint Eastwood, and if Mam caught me, I could blame the family squint and possibly, but not likely, escape her wrath.

"What have I told you about pulling faces? The wind'll blow in the wrong direction one day and it'll stay like that forever."

"Why don't you stick 'r 'manda outside? A stiff breeze could sort out a lot of HER problems."

"You cheeky mare - BEDROOM NOW. And take this with you." Slap, slap. She aims for the back of my legs and, unfortunately, hits the intended target. No wonder I've got knock knees. I may have to revise my naughtiness level, or I'm gonna end up deformed.

I sit and sulk in the bedroom. When I get bored with sulking, I practice face-pulling in the mirror. I achieve a couple of crackers, but don't dare to put my head out of the window. It's a very windy day. No way am I living with one of those monstrosities on me mush, forever.

I can hear the telly on in the living room. The others are watching *Crackerjack*. Bloomin 'eck, I've been in here forever. There was only the test card ... an' her blown glass fish, on the telly when she sent me to my room. Surely it's time to come out now? *Crackerjack's* nearly finished. It must be the 'play' they put on at the end; I can hear Leslie Crowther singing *Purple Haze*. It's horrible to see 'old' people doing pop songs. I cringe. I have been cringing since I could crawl and escaped from my playpen. I crawled into the hallway and stumbled on me mam and dad kissing ... ewww!

Finally, she comes and lets me out.

"I hope you've learnt your lesson, young lady." *What lesson?*

"Don't be cheeky to grown-ups." *Soddin' 'ell, she can read minds!* "I'm putting the tea out. Well, I am once you've come back from the chippy. Here's the note, ask them to wrap the change in it, and don't spill the peas!"

She's not so bad ... sometimes. She gabbles on whilst I'm putting my coat on, something about hitting me 'cos she loves me. Grown-ups are weird!

"Oy, madam. Come here. I've not finished yet." *Hurry up, Woman. Mrs O'Hara goes in there on a Friday and she's got fourteen kids ... .and she won't pay till she's finished a story about the damage they did to her insides. We'll be having our chips for supper if she gets in front of me.*

"There'll be one and tuppence change." *How do mams do that? They're like Einsteins of 'change'!* "YOU can have the tuppence for going."

I can go from 'downhearted' to 'ecstatic' in the blink of an eye. That's the beauty of being a kid.

I'm gonna buy eight - yes eight - black jacks! Or maybe four black jacks and four fruit salads. Or ...

Whatever! I'm gonna buy eight sweets and there's five of us kids. So that's eight sweets for ME and NO sweets for them. She who laughs last and all that.

CHAPTER SIXTEEN
WHAT ACCENT?

Talking about accents ... who'd have thought I'D have an ACCENT? I mean ... I lived in Manchester my whole life. I talked 'normal'.

Granted, my dad talked different to other people. To me, he just talked like Dad.

Foreigners were people from places like Oldham, who got on the 'buzz' and asked you if you were 'orreet.' Yeah I'm fine 'r kid, now get on the next BUS out of town, it's only bees that soddin' buzz round here.

I don't think there's a nicer accent in the whole world. Whenever I'm away from home and I hear that familiar twang, I just know I've found a 'friend'. On the other hand though, there can be some misunderstandings based on how we pronounce certain words. Never mind *The Perils of Pauline.* That's a film that was made before they invented talking, so it might not be the best reference, but I wanted to use the word 'peril' so you're stuck with it. And on that smooth link, may I introduce you to 'The Perils of the Mancunian Accent'?

"Oy! Did you just swear?"

"No, Mam."

"Yes, you bloody well did."

Hypocrite.

"Honest to God, Mam I din't ... 'r 'manda was saying she could go to Nana's whenever she wanted and I said ... 'No you c*nt'."

"ROOM ... NOW."

"What's wrong with your face?"

"I only got nine out of ten in the spelling competition at school." *An' it's YOUR fault.*

"Aw, never mind. Which word did you spell wrong?"

"Birth Sistificate!"

"Well practise for next time. B. i. r. t ... " *I am definitely adopted!*

Oh yes. The Mancunian accent. The most beautiful, if somewhat deceptive, accent in the world. Bogart Hole Clough is one of the local parks. Spent many a summer's day playing in there, and what a surprise it was when I learned to read and realised it wasn't called Bucket-o-Cluff.

Symmetry: the art of harmony and proportion. NOT somewhere where dead people are buried. Neither is 'shintin' a mystic Japanese martial art. It's what you tell the Clubman when he comes to the door.

Not knowing our arse from our elbow doesn't mean we are anatomically challenged. It just relates to the tiny majority of us who are thick, which means stupid for you non-Mancs.

For you lot who may be struggling with our wonderful turns of phrase, here are some examples from the Mancunian dictionary/phrase book, Collyhurst edition:

Are you giving me cheek? Question, to which there is no correct answer. First part of disciplinary routine.

A met meself coming back: I've got so much to do, I'm actually breaking all the laws of physics.

Asbinmanbinmam: A query in regard of rubbish collection times. The most common response being: "What's it got to do with you whether the bin man's been or not. Is it YOUR bin?"

Back entry: Space between 'r house and your house. Great place for kids to play and hide.

Batter: Hit someone, or what a fish wears so you can eat it.

Bazzin: Wonderful. Super, smashing, great (copyright Jim Bowen).

Bokkle: Glass receptacle for storing wet stuff like milk (ew!) or mineral (Yay!).

Brew: Hot drink. Tea, coffee, whatever. A brew's a brew.

Bucket-o-Cluff: Lovely park in North Manchester. Usually seen on maps as Bogart Hole Clough.

Bus: Best method of transport for getting you away from the surrounding *foreign* areas where they call it a 'buzz'.

Butty: Two slices of bread with filling between them, eg jam, brown sauce, sugar. Known as a 'sandwich' anywhere south of Wythenshawe.

Caffolick: Someone who believes in Mary and goes to confession.

Carry on!: Definitely don't carry on. Stop at once.

Chimley: Sits on top of the roof.

Corned beef: Tin meat, says it's beef, but who knows. Ready cooked for going in butties, or can be heated to make corned beef hash (another dish me mam can't cook) OR, to describe the rash you get on your legs if you stand too close to the fire.

Corporation: When ending in 'Pop': A 'witty' retort to a request for some mineral (see below), otherwise the people you pay rent and stuff to.

C*nt: NOT a swear word so offensive that I have to use an asterisk in place of the U. But a way of saying 'could not'. It's YOU with the dirty mind!

Did I eckers like: I did not do that.

Dinner: Meal eaten during the day, about 12-ish. Also known as 'dinnertime' if it's a school day. Lunch is something they do in London (an' they can keep it!).

Dolly Dimple: Someone who is intellectually challenged. Rhyming slang for simple. Good name for any one of my sisters.

Donkey Stone: A tool bought from rag and bone men (when you could have got your CHILD a balloon or windmill ... cruel woman!) which you use to donkey stone (clean) your front step. To impress the neighbours and not have anyone say you're a dirty cow.

Eckers like: That is not so.

Ee yah: Excuse me, can I have your attention for a minute?

Fur coat no knickers: Someone who pretends to have more than they actually do.

Get yer mad up: Become angry.

Gob-sh*te: Big mouth. Usually full of s**t.

I'll put the kettle on: The Mancunian response to war, fire, famine and flood (and Jackie's 'husband' *no ring!* running off with her at number 17).

I'm not as green as I'm cabbage looking: Makes no sense at all, but means 'I'm not as daft as I may look'.

Innit: I agree.

It's bloody cold out today: If said at the bus stop, this is the beginning of a 30 minute (or until the bus arrives, whichever is sooner) conversation with a random stranger in which various subjects, usually operations, cheating husbands and ungrateful kids, are discussed. Otherwise, the standard greeting of one Mancunian to another.

Mard/Mardy/Mardarse: Sensitive, like me.

Mineral: Nectar from the Gods. Comes in many flavours. Dandelion and Burdock is one of the most well-known.

Mingin': Something horrible, eg Mam's ornaments or shoes that are comfy and practical.

Mithered: eg 'I can't be mithered'. This is not interesting to me. I have no enthusiasm for this.

Mrs Woman: Used to attract the attention of someone you don't really know.

Nedache: Pain in the head. Usually caused by kids and eased with phensic and a brew.

Neg: Comes from a chicken.

Nowt: Nothing, I don't owe you nowt.

Oinkment: Creamy medicine for sore fingers and knees. If it's purple it means you have the mange. Or Impetigo as we say to people's faces (but behind their backs it's mange!).

On yer bike: Move away from my doorstep. Get out of here.

Owt: Anything, I don't owe you owt.

Prem: Pretend meat that belongs in the category of mingin'.

Proddycint: Someone who doesn't believe in Mary and doesn't go to confession.

Puddled: Funny (in a not laughing way) in the head.

'R: Our.

Sharra: Coach. Posh form of transport for going to Blackpool.

She looks like piffy on a rock bun: Does she not have a friend or a mirror?

Shintin: Standard doorstep response to Clubmen and her from number 44.

Shit with sugar: Standard Mancunian response to question of what is on the menu for next meal.

Shurrup: Please stop talking.

Shut your cakehole: Be quiet.

Simmetry: Where dead people go.

Sistificate: Proof of birth or exam results.

Skewel: Place of education.

Ta-ra: Goodbye.

Tart: Pastry with jam. Otherwise her at number 44.

Tea: Hot drink that grown-ups drink, even in summer, in the belief that it 'cools you down'. *Normal people and kids go for mineral*. OR Evening meal. Usually eaten just after *The Magic Roundabout* so Mam can watch the news in peace. About six-ish.

There and back to see how far it is: what mams say when you ask them where they are going.

Thingy: Anything or anyone whose name you cannot remember. eg, Who put that 'thingy' on my clean floor? Go and give this note to Mrs 'Thingy' downstairs.

Tight: Mean. Especially with sweets, toys and spends.

Town: No matter what part of the country/world you are in, 'Town' is Manchester city centre.

Who's gonna make me?: Refuse request to stop doing something and ascertain credentials of 'asker' and his/her Army.

Yer dead: You are most likely to be in a spot of trouble with your parent. Other sayings in a similar vein include: 'I'm gonna kill ya' and 'I'll murder that kid'.

* * *

Speaking of accents, there's me, sitting in me granddad's house in Barbados, having gone there for his funeral. So he wasn't there, obviously. Sitting with me dad's family (mine too, of course) being told by my uncle that I HAVE an accent. (The cheek of it! You've not been within a million miles of the CIS MATE. Don't talk to me about accents.)

"Sweety? Seh CAR."

"CAR!"

"A-HA-HA-HA, you is mek me laugh. Yuh hear she? She seh 'CAR'." I know I flippin' did, you told me to! I hope Alzheimer's isn't in me genes! And I don't know what you're finding so bloomin' funny. If you think my talking is so amusing you'd split your sides if you heard Les Dawson.

Actually, it turned out I DID have an affliction.

'Af-flic-tion' ... How my nana loved that word. Everybody she knew had an 'affliction'. Alice the Malice with her 'knees', and we know why, the old tart! Mrs Herbert with her 'husband'. I don't know the nature of his affliction, but according to Nana, she suffered summat chronic with his goings on.

The affliction I suffered from was: 'The further away I get from Manchester, the more Mancunian I become-itis'. So no wonder my poor Bajan relatives struggled to understand me. Anyway, everything for a reason. During the time I lived over there, one of my cousins came over to Manchester to study at our wonderful University. I was able to give her some tips on communicating with the locals. Her favourite bit of advice was:

Don't ask for directions to the ER in Manchester. People will just stand there, waiting for you to ask an actual question.

"Excuse me. ER?"

"Eee-r what?"

All joking aside, I did pick up a slight Bajan accent during the three years I lived there. But four weeks back in Manchester with six kids, one mam and a nana in a two bed terrace, with an outside loo, his was gonna be a 'laugh', and it was like I'd never left. I was soon back to 'skew-el', getting 'dead bored', going meeting 'me mates' at the phone box, our gangland headquarters. Wishing I knew someone with a phone. Not a mobile. Good God, That was Space 1999 s**t! Real life was telling the operator: "I put 2p in and the phone took me money," (whingy voice). Just so you could get a free call to 'Dial-a-Disc'.

Anyway, I started off talking about accents and ended up waffling on about phone boxes. Anyone would think I was stood at a bus stop with me mam. But it goes to show, you can take the girl out of Manchester, but this one'll find her way back. Especially to the paradise that is Collyhurst. No, I'm not being sarcastic! I had some of the best years of my life there.

* * *

I'll never forget the day I found out we were moving to Collyhurst. Not because I was excited. To be honest I didn't have a clue what a 'flat' was. What I remember about that day was, woolly tights had just been invented and Mam had bought me and 'r Karin a pair each.

"Are you sure they should be worn like that 'r Joyce?"

"Yes Mother, they're erm, like 'trews' with feet ... I think!"

So off we trotted to the shops wearing fair isle jumpers and navy blue tights ... nowt else! I still blush when I think of it. Thank God I was too young for cellulite.

We didn't actually buy anything. Me mam just bobbed in and out asking for empty cardboard boxes, and gave the same speech in every shop.

"Mr/Mrs/Smith/Greenshaw/Johnson (she knew 'em all by name), have you got any spare empty boxes? I've got a corporation flat and we're moving out of Mam and Dad's."

Every 'H' was over-emphasised. She has different voices. Shopkeepers get the 'Posh' one. We got the 'Norman Bates' in mother mode one!

"Plenty in the back, luv. Help yourself. The kids look ... er ... nice!" (and severely under-dressed), "Where you moving to?"

"Collyhurst Flats. Got an inside bath."

So has Nana. It's inside the living room.

"We're moving up in the world kids," she says as we arrive at our first proper home. She ain't kidding, it's up two flights of stairs. Ooh, check out that 'chute' ... .that'll be fun. (See Chapter 4)

Our flat is like something from the future. You open a door and there's a toilet. Honestly! INSIDE the house. You open another one and there's a bath, with taps, that water comes out of. We've gone 'Hollywood'. We've got an inside pool.

There are three bedrooms. That should hopefully mean one for Mam and Dad, one for me and one for 'r Karin. The other kid, the fat one, can stay with Nana. But, having said that, Mam's looking a bit chubby, and any time that happens another kid pops up. I think I've worked out where they come from. Mam's always been a bit of a hypocrite (do as I say ... not as I do). I reckon she eats her apple pips, then a tree grows in her tummy and a KID grows on its branches. I'm still working on how they actually get out!

There's only one living room though. Where are we going to sit when we pretend to be posh? And WHERE the 'eck will we set the trifle?

The kitchen, soon to be Mam's permanent residence is ... erm ... a kitchen! The sink is metal, not white like Nana's, and I can't see a mangle. So, I will have to find another form of torture when the brat that is sister number two annoys me. Other than that it's just a boring old 'Don't touch this, don't touch that!' kitchen, except for one thing. There's a big cupboard door and behind that door is ... A

Monster! And he makes horrible monster noises. Especially at night.

"Mam, I'm scared. I don't like it here. Nana's house doesn't make scary noises. I wanna go home."

Number two starts crying, too, mainly 'cos I've just pinched her hard. I need back up!

"Don't be silly you two. This is where we live now. Dad'll be home soon." He was, three days late. But that's another story. How me mam made her first 'Molotov Cocktail'.

"Anyway what's so scary about our lovely new home? Look how lovely everyone round here is."

The whole of the landing had been round earlier with tea and 'something for dinner', and to have a nosy at what we had. Well that's what me mam told Nana!

"Welcome to the neighbourhood chuck ... where've you come from? ... oh, Moston ... me Auntie Gladys ... blah, blah blah!"

"So, how many kids you got?"

"Three and one on the way." *I bloody knew it!*

"Are these them then?" *No missus, we just like sitting in strangers' houses!*

"Yes. This is the eldest 'r Lesley, she'll do anything for anybody ... 'cept ME." She's the reason I'm becoming an expert at 'tutting'. I wish she'd stop talking about me, in front of me, like I'm not even here.

"Oooh a cheeky madam is she? Erm ... .lovely tan they've got."

Me mam's starting to go all 'Clint Eastwood'. The eyes are narrowing. This'll be fun.

"They are 'half-caste'. My HUSBAND is coloured." (She makes him sound like a 'Crayola').

The 'Look' on her face says, 'If you've got a problem with that, I've got a Fist'.

The neighbour beats a hasty retreat.

Anyway, back to the scary noises coming from behind the door in the kitchen. I've already done a little investigating of my own. Well, I cowered at the sink and made me sister open the door. Behind it is A MONSTER. It's a massive metal robot thing, and it growls.

I tell Mam about it. She laughs. This must be what they call 'child abuse', the cruel cow!

"That, my precious darling, is the 'Immersion'. "

Oh Thanks Mam ... that clears everything up!!!!!

She continues. "But I call him Mr Dalek. He's our hot water butler and whenever we want a bath from now on, we won't have to wait for Nana to boil up some water for the tin bath. We just have to ask Mr Dalek and he'll send it by magic to the bathroom."

Well, why didn't she say so in the first place? Having me all scared and that. And he lives here too.

"Do you want to say hello to him?"

"OK. But will you hold my hand, Mam?"

"I'll do more than hold your hand." She picks me up. She's nice and soft and round. I feel much safer now. She opens the cupboard door. I hold on to her a bit more tightly.

"Mr Dalek. I'd like you meet my daughter, Lesley." Mr Dalek rumbles a bit.

"Did you hear that? He likes you. He's saying hello back." I smile, he's nice.

"Hello Mr Dalek."

Not a day went by after that where I didn't say 'Good morning' or 'Good night' to Mr Dalek. He was lovely and gave us lots of hot water. And I loved talking to him. He never ever, ever told anyone else the secrets I confided in him ...

The worst thing about leaving Collyhurst six years later was leaving him. There were six of us by then, and we all cried buckets at having to say goodbye.

It's funny the things that scare you as a kid, but mams are clever. They make it better in special ways, and what they can't fix with a kind word, they can fix with medicine.

CHAPTER SEVENTEEN
MANCUNIAN MEDICINE

"Mam! I've burnt my finger."

"How did you do THAT, you daft sod?"

I've no idea Mother. Could it possibly have anything to do with the rolled up newspaper and box of Swan Vesta you just gave me to get the FIRE going?

"Come here then. Ooooh look at that, a wonder you didn't die." *Sarcky mare!* "Let me put some butter on it. Is that better?" *NO!*

Was butter cheap in the '60s? My mam used it for EVERYTHING.

"Be a luv and make your sister's bottle." (Number four.) I'm far too busy watching *Coronation Street* to deal with these children - who did NOT ask to be born!

"Don't forget, fill it to the number 7 and put 8 scoops in, and a knob of butter for luck." *No wonder she outgrew two and three.*

"It's a lovely sunny day. I want you all outside. Come 'ere, let me rub a bit of butter on your arms. It attracts the vitamin D in the sun." *What school did she go to? Lurpak High?*

Yes butter, and spit on a hanky. Those were part of my mam's medicine cabinet. Only we didn't have a medicine cabinet. We had a cupboard in the kitchen, the highest shelf in the highest cupboard, so we couldn't reach anything and poison ourselves.

"Get this child into theatre stat! She's overdosed on gripe water and calamine lotion. We need to remove her tummy." Well I did watch one or two episodes of Dr. Kildare myself.

I'm telling a bit of a fib about the spit on a hanky though. She never kept that in the cupboard. That was her travelling remedy.

"Come here. How have you managed to get tar on your face whilst we're sat on a bloody bus?" It was on the floor at the bus stop. I was saving it in my pocket. My plan is to give it to 'manda and tell her it's a black jack sweet.

"Don't know Mam. Ew that's horrible." She's just spit on her hanky and rubbed it all over my face. I feel sick. If I get germs it's her fault.

People worldwide hailed the discoveries of penicillin and the polio vaccine. Here in Manchester, we couldn't be mithered with all that. We were too busy celebrating those two greatest of sickness cures, grapes and Lucozade.

Proper poorly people, those at death's door, as me nana put it, had no chance of survival without these miracles. If I ever visited a poorly neighbour with me nana and the Lucozade bottle was empty, you just knew, sometime soon, someone was gonna be making a whole heap of ham butties. Why waste money on another bottle when you know you'll be splashing out on a bottle of sherry in the not too distant future? Just to clear up any confusion for non Mancs. When someone dies, people come to the house of the dead person and eat ham butties, drink sherry and talk about how they're in a better place now. Not if's there's no ham butties, they're not! Ham butties are nirvana.

Once when 'r 'manda fell out of her high chair and banged her head, me mam bought Lucozade. If it hadn't been for the fact she had a fat head, I suppose she could have died. The appearance of the Lucozade did have me wondering if I was gonna gain some bedroom space. But no, she lived (still alive today). What a waste of Lucozade, and just like her to deny her loving family a ham butty. The mean sod!

Grapes too were a sign of impending death. But how nice to visit a nearly dead person and have something to nibble on. You can get sick of apples and don't even go there with oranges. You've got to peel them, pick the pips out and sometimes they were full of blood ... ew!!

"Oh, lucky girl. You've got a blood orange. Eat it all up, it's good for you."

I knew THAT. All things that were good for you looked mingin' but I never heard either Doctors Kildare or Finley once say:

"This man needs a transfusion, stat! Get me a dozen blood oranges!"

What else was in me mam's cupboard? Definitely gripe water and a roll of plaster, for minor cuts and major big mouths. Cod liver oil and malt. Items of torture to be used on a Sunday (I'll tell you more about that in Chapter 28), and Junior Disprin, orange flavoured, which was as close to a sweet as medicine could get.

"Mam, I've got a nedache."

"Go and lie down then." I don't want to lie down. Lying down is bedtime.

"I did lie down (and am lying now as we speak) but it got worster. Can I have a tablet?"

"Well I don't like you taking tablets but if it really hurts?" Why is she looking at me funny?

"It does Mam." Cough, cough.

"A headache that makes you cough? Hmmm. Go on. Just one then."

"Not in your hand madam, in your mouth." Spoilsport. I want to show off first. Run round the living room, waving it in my siblings' faces and watch them go green with envy.

"Thanks Mam."

I'm in the living room in two seconds flat. So I can stick me tongue out and make them lot jealous before it melts.

"Maaaam. Can I have a tablet like 'r Lesley?"

"No you can't, they're not sweets." *Taste like sweets though ... ha, ha.*

"And how do the others know you've got a tablet, young lady?"

('Cos I stuck my tongue in their faces.)

"Don't know, Mam. I think they saw me sucking something."

"You're giving ME a headache now. Stop winding up your sisters. In fact, get out of my sight the lot of you. Bedroom, now!" *How did that happen?*

It ain't funny being stuck in a room with three ugly midgets who blame you for them being there. If looks could kill. But luckily they can't, otherwise I'd have died a million deaths before even reaching the giddy heights of being ten. I give number three a clip round the ear hole, just to remind them who's in charge here. Number two gives her a slap, too. So I slap number two; can't abide bullies!

We settle down and have a dirty look stand-off. Not one of us talking to the other. We're all plotting to 'tell me mam off the others' as soon as we are released from this Alcatraz. I stick my head out of the window once or twice to test the theory mother has that if you pull a face and the wind blows it stays like that. She's a liar.

Me mam's speciality is the 'Dirty Look', and it has more than a few variations. There's the 'We are in a public place, just pretend you're normal for at least 10 minutes. 'Cos if you don't, when we get home you'll know about it.'

Then there's the 'We're passing Collyhurst cop shop on the way home. If you don't pack it in, that's as far as YOU'LL be going Madam,' which is quite similar to her 'I brought you into this world and I can take you out' look.

And that old classic, the 'Show me up one more time and I'll show you a good hiding.' The dirty look however, was more of a deterrent than an actual remedy. So let's get back to the Mancunian medicine list. Vicks was another mainstay of the Mancunian Mam's medicine cabinet, and I'm betting it was cheap, because when you got a sniffle, the whole jar was getting rubbed on you. Chest, back, up your nose, on your nose, behind your ears.

"There you go. That will make you smell better." *Yeah, but every time there's a breeze I feel like I'm in the Antarctic.*

"It stinks, Mam."

"See it's working already. You couldn't even smell bacon earlier, and I know that 'cos you never came anywhere near the kitchen with your Oliver Twist begging bowl when I was making your dad's breakfast."

I do not beg, you cheeky woman. Maybe if you fed us a bit more I wouldn't be starving. How's a kid supposed to survive between breakfast and dinner on one bowl of cereal, two poached eggs and only two and a half rounds of toast? The mid-morning biscuits and milk she chucks at us is a lifesaver. God only knows how we'd manage till dinnertime without it.

She questions us every day in order to ascertain our medical requirements.

"Have you been to the toilet?"

"Yes."

"Wee or poo?" God, the embarrassment, especially in front of your mates.

"Mam (tut)! Both."

"Don't be nowty with me madam, if you don't poo every day, you might die. Next time you go, show me." Ewwwwww!

When you don't 'go', she gets out the syrup of figs, and don't be fooled by the name. It bears no resemblance whatsoever to a syrup pudding. It's thick and brown (not like chocolate either), and it tastes mingin.

But it works! I've learnt to stay within inches of a toilet, the morning after she's shovelled it down me throat.

She's got a horrible remedy for everything. I think she's a bit miffed that headache tablets taste like orange, she'd prefer it if they tasted like cabbage.

I broke my arm at school once. It was Sharon Mulligan's fault, showing off on the 'horse vault' doing handstands and flipping over. That looks easy, I thought. I was wrong. Me mam went mental.

"What the eck were you playing at? Now look at you. God knows what you're gonna wear with that bloody thing on your arm. She was talking about my cast; loved it. It was hard enough to whack someone on the head and still protect me from pain." Come here 'r 'manda. I wanna show you something."

I didn't get done off me mam either. Sick kids get away with murder in our house.

"What do you mean 'r Lesley hit you on the head. She's got a broken arm. She's too poorly to do that and it's not her fault if it makes her funny."

That's right Mam. I'm laughing me head off. It must be terminal.

I'm going off on a tangent again. I was trying to tell you about her medicinal remedy for broken bones, cod liver bloomin' oil.

"It says right on the bottle 'Good for strong bones'. So whilst you're in that thing, you're having a spoonful a day." She truly is an evil genius. That's took the bloody shine off having a broken arm. Can't have no fun me. She always spoils it.

I was careful not to break any bones after that episode. Didn't stop me trying to break anyone else's though. The murderation between me and my sisters got so bad at one time she decided something had to be done.

"Right that's it. I'm sick of you lot fighting all the time. Lesley, you can go and live with Nana for a bit. She's all on her own now that your granddad's gone." (Not to the shops. He'd died.)

Hurrah, going back to me roots. My beloved Moston and my lovely nana.

.

CHAPTER EIGHTEEN
GOING BACK TO MY ROOTS

So it was decided I would live with Nana for a bit. Fine by me and it was the closest I would ever get to my dream of being an only child. I'd lived there for almost the first five years of my life, except for Mam and Dad's forays into the world of rented rooms, which always ended with Mam, me and whoever else was born coming back to Nana's because Dad had buggered up again (usually unpaid rent or a trollop). So Moston was home from home for me. I had friends there and all me nana's mates knew me, unfortunately.

One day, me and a friend (I won't name her, I'm no grass, plus her parents are still alive and the type to hold a grudge) we decided to 'wag it' from school.

That's right. Wag it from school in an area where EVERYONE knew me nana ('Flo' to her friends; 'Cow!' to her enemies).

Flo, who sang like an angel - if that Angel was Hilda Ogden. Flo, who never had a bad word to say about a 'friend' or random innocent person where six would do.

"I wouldn't trust that so-called chiropodist with me cat's claws." We didn't have a cat - a budgie, yes. But a cat? Nope (lies, lies, lies).

Her front door was open from morning till night. She had a 'cup of tea' for anyone. She would send me five streets up to offer workmen a cuppa! From the milkman to the pools man and many a neighbour. Me nana's house was a 'drop-in' centre for the younger readers. A milkman was a man who brought milk to your house and told your nana about his 'getting up to's.'

"What've you been getting up to, Eddie? Were you milking the cow yourself at number 44? You were in there ages."

"Cheeky - I'll tell you though ..."

"Hold on a minute, Eddie," she's doing her wink and aiming her head in my direction, "'r Lesley. Why don't you play with the button tin? Find some jewels."

Why? Does she think the button tin makes me deaf?

"Ok, Nana." This should be interesting; head down, ears open: file under

"Ammunition for the later years."

But back to the "wagging". We went in school. Got our "mark" - clever clogs that we were - and met at the gate at break time.

To the theme of *Mission Impossible* in our heads, we darted down Brookside Road (Moston, NOT Liverpool!) and on to Moston Lane - big mistake!

How were we to know that EVERY pensioner in Moston came out at 11 o'clock? It was like an invasion. They were everywhere: in the shops, on the buses, blocking the pavements with their Tartan shopping trolleys, and I recognised at least a dozen from Nana's "Pop in for a cup of tea - I need some gossip so I can slag you off later" sessions (happy days for a nosy kid).

Oh God! What were we to do? I looked up and saw the Blessed Virgin smiling down on me. You could say our prayers were answered. But I think the fact that we were stood at the gates to Moston Cemetery had a little to do with it. "Quick. In here," I said to my partner in crime. We headed straight for the shrine. Not a penny between us, so we quickly asked the Lord for "tick" as we lit our candles and shivered with fear. Streetwise we most certainly were not.

We spent the next four hours darting between and behind gravestones, to the theme of that "dah, dah, de, dah" music from horror films (in our heads, of course). It's funny how such a lovely place as Moston Cemetery (NOT symmetry, Mam and Nana!) could take on such an ominous and scary atmosphere. When I visited it with my nana (a weekend treat, every weekend), it was lovely. But then again, I was allowed to be there then. This was a Tuesday - bloody pension day!

It was so bloomin' scary, I wouldn't have been surprised if one or two of the dinner ladies had popped up out of an open grave and said "Oy! What you two doing outside my house? Playground, now! I don't get paid to mind you lot in here!" A bit strange were a couple of the dinner ladies in our school. I often wondered if a pathological hatred of kids and love of hair scarves were required qualifications.

"Doris - I don't like them lot from 4C. Hide the cornflake pie, give 'em tapioca. The little sods nicked me roller last week and I couldn't hold my scarf on properly. Got a proper earache on playground duty." One of life's great mysteries to me was, why women, me mam included, wear a head-scarf with one solitary roller on top of their head.

No going back now. We spent the rest of the day hiding and shaking with fear behind a Mr Lombardi's headstone. The Italians had the biggest headstones. Sorry, Irish people. That's a fact.

"How was school?" asked me nana, as I sauntered in casually at 3.45. "Funny thing," (What? - oh sugar, I'm rumbled - I'm DEAD!) "Mrs Taylor swears she saw you in the 'symmetry' when she was visiting her Ronald."

"Nana! She's got cataracts. What would I be doing there on a school day?" (Oh God forgive me, God forgive me!)

"Hmm ... anyway, what do you want for your tea?"

"Prem please I'll go to the butcher's." (Major crush on a lad who works there.)

Only wagged it that one time; weren't worth the stress. Next time I go anywhere it'll be with permission from a grown-up and their blessing, well, sort of. Like the time it was decided I was going to Barbados. Pity it was before the Typically Tropical song - a 'Whoa!' would have fitted brilliantly in this paragraph.

Mam and Dad called me into the living room. They shut the door and told me to sit down. I was convinced they'd found out that some of the Babycham was missing. WELL. If they didn't want me to have Babycham, they shouldn't have stuck it in full view of me, in that box hidden in the gas cupboard where Mam hid her emergency kit (five Park Drive and something alcoholic for when me dad "did her head in"). Anyway, I was twelve by then. Almost grown up. I could be a "Liver Bird' in a few more years. Get me own pad and all that. What was wrong with a bit of Babycham? I stood there defiant and hoping they couldn't see my knocking knees. I was ready for them. Bring it on, parents (now which sister could I blame?)!

"It wasn't me," I began (strike first!). "It was 'r ..."

"Oh, shut up! You don't even know what we want yet," said 'Hitler in a dress'. It WASN'T the Babycham. (Phew!)

"Sit down 'r Lesley," said Mam - me dad NEVER had a Mancunian accent!

"You know your Granddad Mottley in Barbados?" (YES. Of course I do. Went to see him in London, two years ago with Dad, and you're always shoving photos in my face. Are you senile or something?) "Well, he's been very poorly, and he's died."

"Aw, poor Granddad." Awkward pause. I was never much of a crier. I tried thinking of the last scene from *King of Kings* to see if I could squeeze one out. Poor Jeffrey Whatsisname. He was brilliant at being Jesus. She continued, "And Dad has to go to Barbados for the funeral."

(WHAT! Leave us on our own with YOU?) "Anyway, me and Dad had a talk, and we thought it would be a good idea for you to go too. Pay your respects and also get to meet your family."

I'd done two victory laps of the living room before it struck me as not entirely appropriate, in the sad circumstances. "Really?" I said, looking at Dad. He never lied - well, not to his kids. The women in his life were a different matter. But that didn't matter to me.

"Yes, darling," replied my hero. Ha, ha, ha, them lot are gonna be stuck with Mam. Wait till bedtime. They are gonna be fuming with jealousy. "Don't tell your brother and sisters yet." (Spoilsport.) "There's lots to sort out first. Now go on. What you stuck in the house for? Get out and play."

Hmmm. She said don't tell the brats. She didn't mention anything about the rest of the world.

I bombed it round to my current best friend, my namesake, Lesley O. We were a bit more than just good friends, if you get my drift. We'd pricked our thumbs a couple of weeks earlier and were officially "blood sisters."

"I've got some brilliant news!" I was jumping up and down and doing the chicken walk at the same time. Not easy. "My granddad just died!"

"Bit harsh!" she responded.

"NO! Not that he died. That he died in BARBADOS, and I'M going to the funeral. On a PLANE!"

Even better, he died in April. I wouldn't even miss the summer holidays. Me and Lesley O were planning to run away to London in the hols. I hated letting anyone down. A date's a date.

Later on, just before we flew out, me and Lesley said our goodbyes. There were tears and promises to write every week. And I told her to expect me back by the end of July '73. The next time I saw her we both had grandkids.

It was having kids, and more especially grandkids, that made me appreciate me mam more and understand the difference between a love child and a "loved" child. Both of which I was destined to be.

CHAPTER NINETEEN
LOVE CHILD?

As I mentioned in the first chapter, I was born before Mam and Dad were married. However I was too young to remember and didn't find out till I was 12 when some 'caring' individual, or as me mam put it, 'evil old cow' decided to mention it within earshot of me.

"They weren't legal, you know. When SHE was born, Callie was still married to his first wife." All said in a stage whisper - about 60 decibels - and whilst I'm only sat about five bloomin' inches behind her.

"What you saying about MY dad?" I was always defensive of Dad. Whether it be some idiot making racist comments or me mam arguing with him, I was always Team Dad.

"Nowt luv – aw, I didn't see you there." What a liar. I was practically breathing down her neck.

"Anyway, it's true, luv. Your mam and dad couldn't get married until after you were born. But there's nowt wrong with that." Her tone of voice said otherwise.

I sat down and thought about what she said, and suddenly realisation hit me.

Wait a minute. I was born before Mam and Dad were married? And people CAN'T have babies unless they get married. That notion came courtesy of biology lessons with Mam, and my own natural daftness. So that means, one of these people is NOT my parent. I'm betting it's Mam.

I suppose, looking back, I could have just gone and asked her. But that was too simple. Not unlike meself at the time.

"Mam, have you ever been married to anyone else before Dad?"

"I have NOT, you cheeky mare. What do you think I am? Why are you asking anyway?"

Always has to answer a question with another bloomin' question, or two. "Just asking. Has Dad ever been married before?"

"Yes. To someone in Barbados a long time ago." Could have sworn she mumbled "The cow" under her breath. Typical Scorpio, me mam. Even jealous of people he knew before her.

My naïve mind started to go into overdrive. Oh my gawd, it's true. She's not my mam. That explains a lot. I carried on my questioning. Columbo had nowt on me. "And people who are not married can't have babies with each other? That's what YOU say, innit?" I'm not even gonna call her Mam anymore. I'm gonna call her Mrs Woman. But not whilst she's got that spoon in her hand.

"Yes, that is true. Now stop asking so many bloody questions. Can't you find something to do? Why don't you go read your *Bunty*? I only bought it for you yesterday."

"I've read it." (And I'll get my dad to give you the money back. I'm not supposed to take anything from STRANGERS.)

"Well, go and read it again. I bet you haven't read the animal stories. You always say they are boring. I don't know why. I used to love stuff like *Black Beauty* and *Greyfriars Bobby* when I was a kid. You don't take after me at all." No, I don't at all, do I, Mrs Woman - 'cos you're NOT me mam!

My cross questioning over, reality hit me. Aha, I knew it! There was no way this woman could be my real mother. Those were innocent times, and I was innocent to the point of stupid. But at that moment in time I was convinced and my world fell apart for a bit.

I flounced into my bedroom. I was devastated. God, I'm a half-orphan. I pulled out the record player that I got for my 12th birthday and rooted through my record collection until I found the appropriate song. I'd been torn between a few, and my favourite song at the time was *Amazing Grace* but it was the bagpipe version, so no words which was no help at all. I carried on looking. *Son of My Father* by Chicory Tip? Nope, I'm not a boy, but almost appropriate. *Mother of Mine* by Neil Whatsisface - definitely not. Ah! *Love Child*, Diana Ross and the Supremes. Could have been written just for me. I played it till the record wore out, which wasn't helped by me so-called 'Mam' throwing it out of the window. Came in the bedroom. Not a word! Just pulled it off the Dansette and flung it. Then walked out again. Not a word.

I then attempted to go out of the house in no socks and a ripped cardigan. I so WAS that girl in the song. "GET BACK IN HERE NOW MADAM! You are NOT walking the streets with MY name, looking like THAT!"

"I was only going in the garden and it's me dad's name actually!" I shouted back (that's a fib - I mumbled that bit).

"WHAT DID YOU SAY?"

"I didn't say nowt. I hate it here. I can't do anything. You are a wicked stepmother." (Mumbled that bit too - wouldn't do to let her know she'd been rumbled - YET.)

A Nazi who wasn't racist was a fair description of my step-mam. Seems a bit harsh, I know. But if the cap fits. We were 'The State' and she controlled us. I did as I was told. I liked living.

A quick chat with my dad and gales of laughter from him and Mam (turned out she was my real mother) and all was settled.

I soon got over it. It was nothing really. Doesn't even matter nowadays. I pushed it to the furthest corners of my mind, with a reminder to pop it back into me head when she gave her 'saving yourself for marriage' speech. Or indeed any words of advice.

"Good girls don't say rude words and GOOD girls listen to their mams."

"Do GOOD girls have babies before they are married?"

"Are you being cheeky?"

"NO - I'm just asking a question."

"Well, question this!"

"Ow! Mam, that hurt."

"Shurrup and give me back me shoe."

"That's not fair. You threw it."

"Aw, can't you pick one little shoe up? Ee yah! Try a PAIR."

"Ow, Mam! I'm telling me dad."

"Pick the bloody shoes up. Pass them to me. Not with that attitude, madam. Put them down. That's right. AND STOP WHINGIN'. You can tell your dad this!" (slap, slap, slap) "Now BED."

I've got stripes on me legs now. She is so cruel. I'm never gonna talk to her for the rest of my life. Which won't be long if she improves her accuracy at throwing!

* * *

It's funny how when you're a kid, you think everyone else's mam is better than yours. Especially the ones that let their kids do as they like. Or so it seems.

My friend Linda was a bit like that. Linda's mam worked in a factory and her dad worked in the pub - a lot! So Linda had a key to let herself in and was allowed to go in the kitchen any time she wanted. I was so jealous. I wished my mam was like that. It seemed like she was glued to our house. But in later years, I met up with Linda in Middleton Arndale. It seemed like everyone from Collyhurst ended up in Middleton when they pulled our flats down. Good job we weren't all paranoid or there'd have been loads of fights breaking out in Darnhill.

"Hey, didn't you used to live in Collyhurst? Are you following me, you weirdo?"

There we were. Two old childhood friends stood in front of the Wimpy gossiping. We'd turned into our mams!

"How you doing, Linda? It's been years. How's your mam? She was a right laugh, her. Does she still do the night-shift in the pillow factory?"

"Well, if you must know, I don't talk to her any more. Turned out the 'pillow factory' was her spot under the bridge at the side of Piccadilly train station."

"Eh?" I was still in touch with my naïveté at this point.

"She was a prossie - ran off with one of her punters not long after you moved. Me dad was permanently glued to the pub floor, so I got put in care. Not seen her since '71."

"Oh gosh." Too many Enid Blyton books make you talk frightfully middle class. "Well, never mind." (I almost wanted to say: "I'll put the kettle on," but they wouldn't have been best pleased in the Wimpy, as I didn't actually work there.) "We still had some fun, though. Remember us making up recipes from the stuff in your kitchen cupboard, and having the run of the place? No grown-ups. That was great."

"It was loads nicer at your house. Watching telly whilst your mam made us butties."

"Really? I used to pray she'd go out for a bit and give us some peace. But if you remember, she never did."

"I know. You were dead lucky having a mam who cared enough to always be there."

Don't think I ever really looked at it like that until seeing Linda (I changed the name, 'cos it can be a bit embarrassing when everyone knows your mam is a prossie – OK, Louise?). The grass is always greener, they say.

Well, that's a turn up for the books. Not only was I a 'love' child. I was also a loved child. Even if I didn't realise it at the time.

Looking back, though, Mam might not have been one of them lovey-dovey mams, always saying "I love you". But she would kill for us (as well as wanting to kill us, too). In fact, God help anyone who tried to hurt us in any way.

.

CHAPTER TWENTY
RACE WARS

"Mam. Someone just called me a 'black ba ... ' - that rude word we're not allowed to say."

"Well, they are just ignorant, scruffy, dragged-up GITS," - you can tell she's getting her mad up - "with no morals and their kitchen is probably FILTHY!" She's going off on a blinkin' tangent again.

"Go and say to 'em 'AT LEAST I KNOW WHO MY DAD IS,' and tell 'em you're BLOODY PROUD, only don't say 'bloody' - oh yeah," - Come on, woman! They'll be married with kids by the time you finish dictating my witty retort - "and TELL THEM to come and say that to MY bloody face!"

"Me mam sez your mam's a twat. OUCH! Mam, that's me head!" She's gone and followed me outside. How do mams do that silent creeping up behind you thing? Gets me every time.

"Well, I didn't think it was your elbow, and did I tell you to swear?" Not in so many words. But ...

"Oy, face ache!" You can't say that to someone else's kid - oh yeah, you can, it's the '60s. "Go an' tell your mam there's a ship just come in to Salford docks. Why dunt she take you to see your DADS?" Note the emphasis on plural. When Mam insults someone, she does it in style.

All that's going through my head is, Mother, really! Ha ha ha, shown up for life, Sharon Wilson. That's a pseudonym - I wouldn't want to show up the real Sharon Wilson all these years later.

Ten minutes later, bang, bang, bang at the door. Mam opens it with attitude -"WHAT?" Luckily it is Sharon's mam. Imagine the look on his face if it had been the Clubman.

"Well, with that attitude Mrs M, don't be looking for a top-up loan from me this Easter."

I almost wish it was one of my sisters. They've all been playing in the Sand Park and don't know about Mam's 'mood'. If one of them had knocked, there'd have been knocking knees and weak bladders before they'd even got through the hallway. "Why's Mam mad? Have you told off me for something?"

"What did you just say to my Sharon?"

"The TRUTH! Now sod off from my door and go and wash your nets. They're almost as filthy as your kids."

"I'm not standing for that." Here we go.

"Well, f*****g sit, then!" BAM! "Now sod off before I set the dog on you!" Oh my! Sharon's mam wears knickers to her knees. I'd move out the area if I was you, chuck. Your life's about to get miserable. No way am I keeping this to myself. I'll start by telling 'r 'manda. That girl is to keeping secrets what Miles Platting is to Greenery.

Just as an aside: we don't have a dog, but what a good bargaining tool. I'm gonna ask her later, when her mad isn't so far up.

Sharon's mam scarpers, sharpish, mumbling something under her breath. For once I'm kinda glad there's so many kids in our family. Gonna need to walk round in pairs for a bit after this incident. Love my mam. She always sticks up for us. We're gonna have a proper laugh about this - or are we?

"Right. You, madam. Get down off that window sill an' come here." She might call it a window sill. I call it front row seats for the fight of the century.

"Yes, Mam."

"An' wipe that soddin' smirk off your face. What've I told you about bringing trouble to my door?"

I can't bloomin' win! But what's not fair is: she chose to have kids with a black man. Is it OUR fault if people say nasty things? No, missus, it ain't. It's hers an' I'm gonna tell her. Right to her face. One day. Just not today. She's still got her mad up.

Whilst I'm on the subject of race wars, what about sports day at school? I don't know about you, but as far as I'm concerned, if God wanted us to run, he wouldn't have invented buses.

How glad I was when they cancelled the egg and spoon race at my school. No one had a spare egg and my mam for one wasn't letting one of her hard-earned spoons (her words) leave that cutlery drawer. It was the same with the sack race. We were all wearing 'em.

I didn't mind doing dance and movement when we had PE Nowt too taxing about wafting a hanky around to posh music - the kind with no words. But all that going outside in your vest and knickers, and running round in circles? Well, I wasn't impressed. But I'd have to like it or lump it. Unless I used my talent for reading and writing, to forge notes from me mam. What could go wrong?

"Dear Mrs Smith, Our Lesley can't do PE today. She has a poorly knee. Love from Mrs Mottley"

"Thank you, Lesley. Your mother is a very affectionate person, isn't she?"

"Erm ... .yes, suppose so." Note to self: don't put 'love' on the next one.

"OK then, whilst the others are doing ten laps of the playground, you can tidy up the rings and balls in the gym. Right, you lot, outside now. I can't believe you're all scared of a bit of rain. You're in Manchester. Get used to it!"

Ah, the lovely warm gym, which was also used for assembly and dinner time. If I play my cards right here, the dinner ladies will see what a lovely helpful girl I am and give me an extra big piece of cornflake pie.

"Miss, should I help you put the water jugs on the table?" Simper, simper, grovel, grovel.

"Why? What you doing in here anyway?" God. She's a suspicious one.

"I've got a poorly knee. So I can't do PE and Miss gave me some jobs to do, but I've finished now. So can I help you?" Head cocked to one side. Puppy dog eyes.

"Ooh, aren't you luverly." Ya fink? "Go on, then. Two jugs per table and mind you, don't spill 'em."

I got seconds of cornflake pie that day, and one of them was a corner piece. Result!

This note writing lark is easy. We've got rounders next week. Outside! And it's November.

"Mrs Smith, Lesley can't do PE this week because she has a poorly arm. Thank you kindly, Mrs Mottley (her mam)."

I think I'll be a secretary when I grow up. I'm good at this letter writing lark, and I've still got a few more limbs to go. So I reckon I can get out of PE till the weather warms up.

"You've been in the wars a bit recently. Is everything alright at home?"

"Yes, Miss."

"OK. You can read in the library." Hurrah! "Are you on the phone at home?"

"No, Miss." What a nosey cow! Have YOU got an inside toilet? How would you like it if people asked you your personal business? Anyway, we're on the waiting list for a phone, me mam says.

"Come and see me at home time. I want to give you a note to take home to your mother."

"OK, miss. I'll come as soon as the bell goes."

No I blinkin' well won't. I'm off, Missus. It's Friday and we're breaking up today. By the time I come back you'll have forgotten. Anyway, what you sending me mam notes for? Are you two bezzie mates or something?

Home time comes. Miss is waiting for me at the door. Got trust issues have some people. I said I'd come to staffroom. Need to practice my 'sincere' smile more.

"Give this to your mam." She's sealed it in a soddin' envelope. I wonder what's in it? If Mam was the decent type she'd sod off out for a bit and leave me in the house alone. Then I could steam it open. Like she does with Dad's letters (oh yes ... I've seen you Mother). But fat chance of that. She's always in doing the easy stuff like looking after teeny babies. How hard is that? Get a job, Woman. Like Linda's mam, slaving away in that pillow factory every night!

"OK, Miss. See you after the holidays."

"I hope so, love." Why is she ruffling my hair and looking at me like that? She's still rabbiting on, something about children at risk - has 'r 'manda been telling her I hit her? Such a likkle liar. Am gonna batter that kid after. "Never forget ... There are people who can help."

(Did she just sniffle?) "Er ... OK, Miss. Thank you ... bye." I'm off like a shot. What a weirdo.

By the time I've got home I've forgotten all about the note. I've got just enough time to have my biscuits and drink (Mam always gives us something to tide us over till tea time) before *The Tomorrow People* starts. It's about kids who can go into the future and one of 'em is black too. You didn't get too many black people on telly in them days so you take what you can get. Up to now we've been stuck with Lieutenant Uhurhu and occasionally Kenny Lynch. *The Black and White Minstrel Show* doesn't count!

I can hear Mam moaning in the hallway, "Bloody 'ell, don't none of you kids know what a coat rack is?" We do but the corporation doesn't exactly do child-friendly fittings. It's about ten feet off the ground. I've long since come to accept I'm not gonna be a basketball player. I give it two jumps and if I don't hit the hook, I use the floor. Anyway, why have kids if you're not prepared to pick up after them?

Guess what? I'd completely forgot about the note in my pocket. It's dead quiet in the kitchen, but I'm not paying any attention to Mam anyway. *The Tomorrow*

People has just ended and I'm settling down to an episode of *Magpie - Blue Peter* for working class kids.

Suddenly I hear her dulcet tones. "LESLEY DONNA MARIA SMARTARSE MOTTLEY. Get your backside in this kitchen now!" What've I done now?

"Can I just see the end of *Mag - ...*"

"KITCHEN NOW!" Blinkin' 'eck, don't get your knickers in a twist.

She's sat at the table with a piece of paper in her hands. I bet she's skint and wants me to go to the shop with a note ... Note? Oh God, she's got the school note. I can feel the blood leaving my face. I've not even seen it. So I've not got a clue what I've got to deny.

"Do you need me to go to the shop, Mam?" Worth a try. "If you want me to, I will. Should I give the baby a bokkle? I don't mind." I'm on full 'creep' mode. She remains silent. She only does silent when it's proper serious.

"How's school?"

"Erm, great. I got top marks in the spelling competition again." Is she impressed? Nope, don't think so.

"What about sports?" Oh God, if you help me out right now, I promise I'll never be bad again. Please, please, please. Hail Mary amen.

"Mam, I know what you're thinking, but -"

"No. I don't think you do. 'Cos if you did, you'd be s*****g bricks right now." Not so posh now, are you? "This letter your teacher sent is telling me that someone from the welfare is going to pay me a visit. 'COS THEY'RE CONCERNED YOU'RE BEING PHYSICALLY ABUSED. We don't want them to have a wasted journey, do we? Oy! Get back here, you little sod!"

No bloody fear. I've bombed it. I'm gonna hide in the Sand Park till I see Dad's Humber pull up and it's right next door to the Cop Shop too. Just in case I need protection. God knows I'm gonna need it, if she gets her hands on me whilst she's in that mood. How I am I gonna get out of this? I'll have to live in the park forever ... Why, oh why did I write them notes? Too bloody clever for me own good. Aw, I'm dead sorry, Mam. I wanna come home ... But, on the other hand, living in a park? Hmm. Interesting. Built in swings ... I can sleep on the round-a-bout. The one here is faster, but the one in Queens Park is comfier and there's a toilet in the library. Decisions, decisions ... which park to choose?

CHAPTER TWENTY-ONE
THERE'S LOADS OF PARKS NEAR COLLYHURST

Just so you know, I didn't have to live in a park. Mam got a bit worried and sent 'r Karin to fetch me. Not that that was a comfort.

"You are so dead when you get home. Mam said to tell you it was alright, so you'd come home, but you are so dead." Shurrup, you cow.

"What did she EXACTLY say?"

"She said 'Go and tell that big lump of conniving connivingness to get her backside in the house now.' You're so dead, ha ha ha ... Oh yeah, she also said she wasn't mad at you, but I wouldn't believe that. She even shouted at 'r Wayne."

Now that is serious! She never shouts at that kid. I'm doomed. But it's starting to get dark, and the prospect of living in the park doesn't seem so enticing. The bushes look creepy at night, and the slide starts to look like a giant cat with its back arched. Time to face Mam.

Sometimes, doing the baddest things gets the most reasonable response from mam. She gave me a good talking to, but she also gave me a lovely cuddle and made me some drinking chocolate. Well, not just me. All of us, and she put a square of real chocolate on the top. Lovely.

And the next day I was back in the park. This time the bushes looked like dens and the slide looked like a slide.

Aren't we lucky living in Manchester? We have loads of parks; it's like being in the country, but with railings.

When I lived in Collyhurst you could stand on the landing, spit and hit a park ... or the woman on the landing below, on occasion (deny, deny, deny).

There was the Sand Park. The one closest to our house. I suppose you could call it our daily park. Miles from a beach and more grit than sand, but WHAT a roundabout. Get that thing going fast enough and the look of terror on a sister's face? Well, it made the effort of turning it well worth it, and you got a bigger share of the Angel Delight 'cos they was too sick to eat any.

"What's up with 'r 'manda?"

"Don't know, Mam. She was fine at the park. Can I have her Angel Delight?"

Then there was Queens Park. Had it all, playground, museum, and not a boring one either. This one had doll's houses. Dead posh as well, and kids could go in on their own! If it started raining, there was a library too, just outside the park. You could sit down, read a bit of Enid Blyton whilst you waited for the rain to stop. Then get back to your picnic, with lashings and lashings of salad cream butties and corporation pop. I reckon the people who built parks in Manchester were dead clever, possibly kids.

The poshest one, though - it had a lake with boats, that we could never afford to go on - was Bogart Hole Clough. Clough is just a posher way to say park and bogart is ... something to do with bogarts. That was the day out with Nana, park. Not Granddad, he had his funny leg He could only get a far as the Bowling Green near the Ben Brierley Pub, and that wasn't even a proper park. What kind of park tells kids to stay off the grass, and lets old people throw heavy balls on it?

Being a kid, though, the time comes when you want new experiences. You can sometimes get bored with this treasure surrounding you.

"Mam, I'm bored ... and before you ask, my bedroom IS tidy. "

"Go to the Sand Park. "

"Aw, Mam, I went there yesterday and the day before. "

"Well, go to Queens Park then. You can do me a favour too and pop in the hardware on your way there. Give 'em some money off the glass fish I've got on lay away." Oh! But I can't have this week's *Bunty* 'cos you're skint ... liar.

"I went there on Monday, Mam. It's closed anyway. They are painting the railings."

She never comes out the kitchen ... not like she's gonna check. "Really? Closed, is it? I'll have a look when I go to the hardware myself."

"I'll go, Mam. Not to the park, 'cos it really is closed." Gulp. "But I'll go to the shop for you 'cos I want to be kind to you, 'cos you're dead busy and ever such a good mam."

(I think she fell for it.)

"Hmmm. Right, take me card, and DON'T lose it. Tell em it's for Mrs Mockley. I'll be in with the final payment next week. Gonna look lovely on the window sill, is that fish."

We're called MOTTLEY, Woman! God, she can't even say her own name properly ... and why would you put a fish on the window sill what your kids use as extra seating, 'cos you're too tight to get a bigger settee? That's just asking for trouble. Well, don't come crying to me when it gets broke. Next Sunday if I can help it ... and find someone else to blame.

"OK, Mam. Mam? Seeing as I'm going up there, can I go to Bogart Hole Clough with Yvonne Tompkins? Please Mam? Yvonne's allowed."

"OK then. But I want you back in the house by five."

"OK."

"How will you know when it's time to come home?" Well, you could help and buy me a watch!

"I'll ask a Lady."

"Good girl. Now off you go ... and don't lose that money."

I wouldn't dare. I dropped tuppence down a grid in '63. Never heard the last of it. "No, you can't have a bar of chocolate/comic/balloon/windmill! I'm TUPPENCE short! You can have two black jacks, an' be grateful I'm not one of those mams who puts their kids in a HOME!"

Talk about holding a grudge!

Anyway. Off to call for Yvonne. Her big brother's coming, too. That means we can be cocky if we want with other kids. But it also means we have to go up to girls and tell them, "That lad over there sez he fancies you." What's that about? I will never ever ever 'fancy' a BOY! Eww! Me little brother's a boy and talk about annoying. When I grow up I'm moving somewhere where there is none.

Yvonne and her brother Frank are waiting for me.

"We've got sherbet mixed with water and we've nicked some of our mam's After Eights. What did you get?"

I proudly show them four butties. Two with salad cream and two with sugar. We are gonna have a feast, especially with them After Eights. My mam says they're only for grown-ups and you can only eat them at night. Who cares? Am a rebel me though. There's at least two after eights with my name on em, and I'm gonna eat mine at four. 'Cos I'm big and hard and she'll never know. What she don't know can't hurt me.

We set off up Rochdale Road. It's a bit of a walk but there's loads to see and do on the way. Railings to be rattled. With an appropriate stick, and no adult to say, "Shurrup, you're giving me a nedache!" Houses to 'knock a door run.'

"Go on, Lesley, I dare ya to knock on that door there."

"Why that one?"

"'Cos that one is where Jack the Ripper's mam lives."

A child with any sense would have realised that Jack the Ripper's mam was dead by now. 'Cos he comes from the olden days, so bloomin' 'eck, she must have come from even more olden days. I however was NOT a child with sense. I was a child who didn't want to be called chicken.

"OK, I'll do it ... I'm not scared. But you'd better wait for me."

"Yeah ... course we will ... go on then."

"I AM. I'm just getting me mad up in case she tries to kill me. So I can kill her back."

Frank has walked off ahead of us mumbling something about idiots. I have a quick look round but can't see any. No wonder he has to wear glasses.

I bang on the door and bomb it. I realise that Frank and Yvonne have bombed it too. The traitors.

By the time I catch up with them they are both laughing their heads off. Not literally, but I wish!

We're nearly by the side of Bogart Hole Clough by now.

"Who wants a race to the gates?" I say. I didn't smoke in them days so running was quite easy.

"Actually we're not going to this park," said Frank. "We are going to Eatin' Park."

Oh my Gawd. Another park and called Eatin'. Good bloody job we'd brought a picnic.

I was knackered by the time we got there, but it was worth it. There was a zoo. Not a proper one with elephants and tigers and stuff, but there were some goats and a rabbit. You didn't see many goats on Thornton Street North. You saw rabbits, but usually in a pie. So it was pretty good. There were swings, too, and loads of secret paths and bushes to explore. We had a great time. Eventually we decided to find out the time.

We couldn't see any women. But there was a man with a dog; close enough.

"Have you got the right time, mister?"

"No but I can let you have the wrong time half price." Every fella round here thinks he's a bleedin' comedian. "It's quarter to five, Chuck."

Time to get off. Don't want to go but can't wait to tell my sisters about this new park. Not gonna tell them where it is though. They're not coming ... ever! And it's nearly the time Mam said to be home.

Is it me? Or does it always feel longer coming back than going? That journey home seemed to take ages. Every time we turned a corner, hoping to see a familiar landmark like the war memorial or May's, we were faced by rows and rows of posh houses. Eventually, though, we come to Harpurhey Baths (if only we had our costumes - next time). We know we've got a bit of a walk still to go but it's nice to be in familiar surroundings, especially as it was getting dark now.

We get further down Rochdale Road. More near to home. We see a lady stood on the corner near May's. She's all dressed up and has loads of makeup on. I wonder if to tell her what my nana told me about swinging a handbag, but a car pulls up and she gets in.

We're nearly home now. That's funny, why are all the shops shut? We see another lady coming towards us. "Excuse me, missus. Can you tell us the time?"

"It's half past seven, luv. "

"Thank you. "My voice has gone several degrees higher. Any higher and Lassie would turn up to see if he could help. I am so dead ... again!

Have you ever seen a grown-up trying to deal with a combination of relief and desire for vengeance? Not nice at all. Vengeance almost always gets the upper hand ... an' vengeance hurts.

When I do finally show my face, she threatens to take me to some shop where I can be swapped for a hostess trolley or a chocolate tea-pot. Either of which she's screaming is an improvement on me. Never heard of no such shop. But there's a shop for everything, so I wouldn't be surprised.

CHAPTER TWENTY-TWO
YOU CAN'T BUY PREM IN THE PAPERSHOP

"Get your coats on. We're going to the shops." Why? I'm watching *Mary, Mungo and Midge*. It's one of the first gritty urban dramas to be seen on telly. Mary, Mungo and the other one live in a block of flats. Only it's a cartoon ... well, sort of. It's an English cartoon. Which means it's not like a proper cartoon. A proper cartoon is Tom and Jerry, or Bugs Bunny. They walk like people (Yes, I know they're animals, but you get my point?). Mary doesn't so much move as bob along. It's like her head is doing that Egyptian Sand Dance, whilst the rest of her body is dead still.

Mam's not having it though. "It's like Mother Hubbard's kitchen in there. I can't believe the amount of food you gannets get through."

Oh, sorry! Excuse us for eating. When you bring the next lot of shopping home, we'll just sit and look at it. OK?

"Where we going?"

"There and back to see how long it is. I just told ya. We're going to the shops."

"No. I meant which shop?"

If it's just downstairs to the shops we live above, I can get away with just wearing me poncho and I'll be back in plenty of time for *Fingermouse*. But if it's up the road, all hope is lost, and I'd better wear the duffel.

"We're going to the shops on Rochdale Road. I need some good, decent veg."

If there's even such a thing as 'good' veg, it won't be decent by the time she's finished cooking it.

No such thing as a supermarket like Asda when I was a kid. Well, there might have been, but it was either too far on the bus or my mam just liked going in TWENTY different shops. I'm going with the latter. The woman loved shops (especially ornament ones), and in fairness, for some of the stuff that Dad cooked (hurrah) we had to go a little further afield than Queens Road.

Nowadays you can buy everything under one roof. But back then the shopkeeper would have thought you were mad if you'd said:

"That's right, Mr Jones. 10 Embassy, the *Manchester Evening News* ... and have you got any Prem?"

So duffel coat it was. Twenty minutes later, after me mam has checked the gas for the hundredth time, we're ready for the off. One mad woman and three kids (two idiots and ME) off to do shopping.

We don't need any stuff for Dad today, so it's a walk down Rochdale Road. She's just counted the money in her purse and has a smile on her face, so I know we're not going to Mays the pawnshop first.

"Hold your sisters' hands whilst we cross this road. Karin and 'manda, get on either side of 'r Lesley and hold tight."

"Ow, Mam, she's squeezing me hand tight!"

"What you doing to 'r 'manda?"

"You just said to hold tight. Is it my fault she's mard?" Wait till I get that kid home ... I'll show her 'squeeze' ... she's sleeping in her shitty Tippy Tumbles pram tonight.

Butcher's first.

"Can we have a chicken, Mam?"

Both her and the butcher burst out laughing. Weirdos.

"It's Tuesday, luv. No one has chicken on a Tuesday. Give us a pound of stewing meat, George, and 10 rashers of that bacon."

"Can we have pork chops, then?"

"Have you got pork chop money? No, you haven't."

(Why you askin' then if you know the answer ... and do you give me any money? No, you don't, you tight cow. God, I'm turning into her. I just did it myself. Asked a question then answered it. I'm doomed.)

"I'll be in on Saturday for me chicken."

"I'll save you a big one, pet. For your little army, 'ere, and I see there's another one on the way too."

Well, thanks for letting me know! It's a rum do when you have to be informed by the soddin' butcher that you're gonna be a big sister ... AGAIN (at the time of this event I hadn't worked out the connection between fat tummies and babies).

Greengrocer's next. Tangerines, grapes, melons. All lovely stuff that we aren't getting. Apples and oranges, that's the fruit we have to have. Cheap and nutritious, according to me mam. 'Cheap' is the deal maker for her.

"Got some lovely blood oranges going cheap, luv."

"I'll take 'em." And I'll leave 'em, thank you very much. Blood? In an orange? I think not.

Onions, carrots and potatoes next. Another week, another pan of stew (sigh). Wait a minute, though. She's buying grapes. Is someone ill?

"Give me a bunch of them black grapes ... No, the smallest one. Me mam's neighbour is poorly, but I've been told she's at death's door, so I don't want to waste me money. A friend of mine did that recently. Bought a massive big bunch. Turned up at the wake a few days later and there they were, taking pride of place in the centre of the sideboard, right behind the ham butties. The cheek of it!"

What I'd do is take the bunch, do the visit and what they don't eat whilst I'm there, bring home with me. Grown-ups have no sense.

Oooh we're gonna pass the cake shop next.

"Mam, can we have ..."

"I haven't got cake shop money. There's plenty of biscuits in the cupboard at home, so stop moaning."

Bloomin' rich tea and a few bourbons. I want a trifle or anything with a cherry on top.

"Aw, but Mam. I hate rich tea. They're not even proper biscuits. They're like crackers that are a little bit sweet."

"I'll tell you what you can have. You can have piffy on a rock bun! Now pick your face up off the floor. Stop dragging your feet and hold these spuds. Me feet are killing me." And your blatant cruelty is killing me.

Past the cake shop we go. Three sad children and Hitler in a dress. _Quelle surprise_ (there's a French phrase book in me junior encyclopaedia), we're going in the ornament shop ... no money for cake. Plenty for ceramics.

"Hiya, Joyce."

"Hiya, Gladys."

They see that much of each other; not only are they on first name terms,

Gladys thinks she can touch us.

"And how are you, chubby cheeks?" Are you calling me fat, Missus? And stop pinching me face.

I remain silent with a scowl on my face.

"Oh don't mind her, Gladys. She's got a face like a slapped arse 'cos she can't have a trifle from next door. But if you buy for one you've got to buy for all. Right here's another shilling off my crinoline lady statue. How much do I owe now?"

"Only another two bob, luv, and it's all yours. "

"I'm tempted to get it now." NOOOOO! Get trifles! "No, I'll leave it. I'll definitely have it next week, though. Better get this lot home now. Want them fed and watered before *Coronation Street* starts."

They both start laughing. God only knows why. I've not heard her say nowt funny since we stepped out the door. Come to think about it, I've not heard her say anything funny me whole life.

She calls in at the cobbler's to pick up my school shoes. Apparently I walk 'funny' so the cobbler put these little bits of metal on the side of each heel. They click and I can pretend to be a tap dancer. 'Funny' feet are a blessing in disguise. I love the smell and look of the cobbler's (not as much as the cake shop though). It's all dark brown and smells lovely. So comforting.

Just the paper shop now. The bell rings when we enter and the lady comes out from behind a door made of ribbons. We used to have one hanging on the front door in the summer holidays. But Mam had to get rid of it because we drove her bloody mad, messing with it.

"It is not a soddin' Maypole and stop wafting in and bloody out of it ... an' it's not long hair neither. So stop trying to wear it like a wig." Spoilsport.

We had to go back to using a normal door ... and Mam's traditional doorstep greeting.

"Next time you come in you're staying in. I'm sick of this door knocking every five minutes."

That's what you have to put up with when you play out. Of course you want to play out. But you also want to be able to come in. For such things as the toilet or a butty or the toilet again. All things essential to a kid's existence. Personally I didn't know what her problem was. The kitchen was right next to the front door. It's not like she had to walk miles. Even easier, she could have put the catch off on the door, so we could come and go whenever we wanted. That suggestion was met with the following:

"And let you walk in and out whenever you want?" Well, that's the general idea. "I'd have nothing left in me hallway." I once borrowed the hall mirror. Me mate's brother was in the Boy Scouts and he told us how to send signals with a mirror and the sun. Fascinating stuff, and did you know that you can also use a mirror to make fire? I didn't ... not till the day I 'borrowed' it and set fire to a piece of paper on the ground. I was so surprised I dropped the mirror and now she never lets me hear the end of it. One time!

Digressing again. Sorry, where was I? Oh yeah. Waiting to be served in the paper shop and sulking, 'cos I know it's not even worth asking for any sweets. Not whilst she's in a mood. Which she is.

"Can I have five Park Drive, please, and a box of matches?"

"Is that it, luv?"

"I'll take a *Woman's Own* ... and give me a quarter of pear drops for these little miseries."

They both laugh. I'm so happy I wanna do a conga round the shop. But it means touching a sister and I can't stand 'em. I only hold their hands 'cos I'm forced to.

The paper shop is one of the row of shops underneath where we live. Two minutes and we're home. Coats off, fire going and telly on. It's too late for *Fingermouse* but just in time for *White Horses*. Mam settles us on the settee and shares out the pear drops.

"One for you, one for you, one for you. Two for you ..."

I end up with four pear drops. I pop one in my mouth with the intention of sucking it till it's tiny, but I forget and a few minutes later start crunching. I tell myself I'll eat another two and save one for school. School doesn't start back for another week ... that pear drop isn't gonna make it!

.

CHAPTER TWENTY-THREE
THE JOYS OF SCHOOL

Apart from PE, I loved school.

When I look back, it seems to me I wasn't praised enough for my time management skills. In fact, I wasn't praised much at all. But that's a Mancunian Mam for you. Spare the praise or spoil the kid.

Look at all the stuff, or mischief if you want to put it that way, that I got up to and I still had time to switch personalities and attend school as a proper goody two shoes. Me mam's face at parents' evenings was always a sight to behold.

"She reads cornflakes boxes ... is that normal?"

"Oh yes Mrs Mottley. We encourage the children to read. Lesley is the best reader in her class and she's ever such a helpful child too."

"Helpful?"

"First one to put her hand up when I need help and always approaches tasks with a smile."

"Erm ... can I just check ... we are talking about my LESLEY?"

"Yes Mrs Mottley. She's a credit to you."

"Well she doesn't do nowt for me." *That's 'cos you're a mam and I didn't ask to be born.*

I was a great reader and me mam ain't lying when she tells people I could read at the age of two. I was so far ahead when I started in infants one, that they had to give me special permission to go in the junior section of the school library. My Peter and Jane book was 127B.

"See Jane getting ready for her wedding."

"Where is Peter?"

"There he is, in Jane's dress."

"Peter looks awkward. Jane looks devastated."

"Mother has fainted. Father is looking for his gun."

Ah schooldays. Happiest days of my life. Learning stuff. A mid-morning snack of milk and biscuits. Playtimes and a decent bit of dinner. What more could a child ask for? Troy Tempest as head teacher would have been nice, but you can't have everything. Like I said though, I absolutely loved school. But first I had to get there, and in all honesty this is where Mam came into her own. Super organised was me mam. I didn't appreciate it then, but when I look back ...

"Right! Come on you lot. Time to get up for school."

"I'm tired."

"You've been asleep for 10 hours don't be daft." She was right too. Bedtime was 6 pm on a school day.

"I don't want to get out of bed, it's cold."

"The fire's on and I've made porridge. Yours is in the big bowl." Oh thanks, Mother Bear. I'm coming. Mam makes lovely porridge.

She's right. It's lovely and toasty warm in the living room, and she lets me eat my porridge in front of the fire. The bathroom however is another thing, bloody freezing in there. So on winter days, Mam brings a bowl of hot water in the living room and does us a top and tail. All our clothes are laid out in a row on top of the fireguard. Three rows set out in the order we get dressed.

Vest, knickers and socks or tights first. Then dress or skirt; we never wore trousers for school 'cept Wayne, obviously. Cardi or jumper, all warmed by the heat of the fire blazing in the hearth. Lovely.

"Right. Coats on."

"Mam I can't breathe when you button the top one."

"Well I'd rather you couldn't breathe than catch your death from a chill round your neck." Makes sense I suppose, in her world!

"I've done you a hard-boiled egg for your break. Put it in your pocket whilst it's nice and hot. You can hold on to it on the way to keep your hands warm."

Normal mams give their kids gloves. She does too. The egg is her idea of a bonus. But when I think of it now - aw, how sweet. Not being old enough, however, at the time to appreciate this token of motherly love I just felt shown up. Still it's better than the times she'd turn up with hot Bovril in a flask at playtime.

"Is that your mam?"

"Where?"

"There. At the fence. I think she's shouting you."

Oh God. What does she want?

"Hiya, Mam ... what?" (Said in my cockiest 'I know I'm safe 'cos there's a fence between us' voice.)

"I've brought you something hot to drink. It's perishing out here today ... ee yah get some of this down you."

It's nice but bloody 'eck I'm gonna suffer later. I can see Sharon Walker, the official class bully, out of the corner of my eye. Thanks a lot, Mam.

I wonder sometimes if the chap who wrote *The Waltons* ever lived near us.

School was great though, and I really mean that, especially primary school. I was lucky enough to go to the same one from Infants 1 to Junior 4, St. James Primary just behind Mays pawnshop. Talk about convenient for me mam.

I loved to learn stuff. Which is NOT the same as being nosy, for you jokers reading this. Yes, I mean you 'r Karin, and I also loved school dinners. Mind you, me mam hadn't exactly set the bar high with her efforts.

Cornflake pie, mashed potato in the shape of a perfectly round ball with NO lumpy bits, Mother, and that stuff you told us about the lumps being the bits that contained all the goodness, that was a lie! Cheese and onion pie. Homemade or school made, but by clever dinner ladies. I can't think of anything I didn't like about school dinners, except sago. I must have repressed the memory of that one. But it's all coming back to me now. Frog spawn ... yuck. When that was on the menu I certainly wasn't having a pudding.

In infants you also got milk in a little bottle with a straw at playtime, and there were wonderful things to play with like the Wendy house and sand pit. The more I think about it the more I realise school was like a day at Disneyland. Nowadays my neighbour has got his own bouncy castle and massive tree house for his kids, but in them days we had nowt like that at home, so school was a bit of a treat.

I think that my absolute favourite place in the whole school, except for the hall at dinnertime, was the school library. I wasn't fibbing about being able to read at the age of two. I found the alphabet as easy as A B C (do you see what I did there?), and I just took to words and reading like a duck to an orange. At reading time during my time in the Infants, I was allowed to go to the school library and choose my own book to read. By the time I got into junior one, I think I'd gone through every Enid Blyton book they possessed. I love Enid Blyton books. It's a shame political correctness has gone a bit bananas (can I say that?) - after all, they were of their time, and 'colonial' thinking was the way it was. To be honest, I'd pay more attention to the descriptions of food with lashings and lashings of ginger beer and heaps of yummy cakes, then I did to the berating of 'Johnny Foreigner'. (Can I say THAT?) I also used to love Road Runner cartoons on telly, but to this day I have never attempted to purchase a bomb from ACME and tried to kill anyone. Kids are not daft you know.

I wasn't too good at sums, but that didn't really bother me, except when I got to high school; double maths was a killer. The year after I left school, someone invented calculators ... soddin' typical! Everything else was brilliant though, and I learned some really good skills, too. Like baking. My rock cakes were authentic. They tasted just like rocks. We did knitting and sewing too whilst the boys did woodwork and metalwork. How sexist, I hear you say. Well not really to us at the time. I, for one, would have rather sat down doing daisy stitch than sawing a big lump of wood, and all these skills saved me a fortune in Mother's Day and birthday presents.

"Happy birthday, Mam."

"Ta, what is it?" How bloomin' offensive. Is she blind?

"It's a crocheted thingy. You can put one of your (many) ornaments on it. The holes are deliberate (well some are); it's the pattern."

"Oh, I see now. It's lovely." (I know!)

"Happy Mother's Day, Mam."

"Aw that's lovely. A gingham tablecloth."

"It's NOT a tablecloth. It's a wraparound midi skirt. See, there's another button ... for if you are ... erm ... fatter sometimes." (The baby making was still an ongoing thing.)

"Well, it's lovely. I'll save it for best." She's got her 80th coming up in four years. I reckon that's the 'best' she's saving it for.

I got really good at knitting, though, and in later years she allowed the Chosen One to wear a cable knit jumper I had made ... in public. If that's not approval, I don't know what is.

I really enjoyed learning stuff, too, and loved coming home and passing on my new-found knowledge.

"Mam, did you know that we have fireworks 'cos a man called Guy Fawkes tried to blow up the corporation?"

"I'n't that a coincidence, 'cos we do 'Penny for the Guy' on the very same day. Do you want a bowl of cornflakes to keep you going till tea time?" Gawd stay in the kitchen, Woman ... it's safer.

Playtime was good, too. Sometimes one of us brought in elastics or a skipping rope - great fun. We had playground monitors - dinner ladies with a coat and whistle. Peter Kay covers the subject of 'dinner ladies' in his excellent autobiography and I can't really add anything to what he had to say other than 'Them Bolton dinner ladies had dopplegangers in Collyhurst and Moston'.

Another thing I learnt in school was teamwork and loyalty. At St. James' we had "houses" when you went into Junior 1. The teacher allocated you to a house and throughout the year your house achieved points for winning at games and stuff. At the end of the year, the house with the most points got a shield with their name on it. Nowt like a bit of healthy competition.

Each house had a colour associated with it. If I recall correctly, and please feel free to correct me if I'm wrong, (not that I care, the book's already gone to print,) they were Livingstone - Red, Scott - Blue, Nelson - Green and Nightingale - Yellow.

Nobody really wanted to be in Nightingale ... ew yellow, like a cowardly custard. I ended up in Nelson, which was OK I'd have been gutted if I had got Livingstone, 'cos I was a born Blue. Me and Granddad wouldn't even eat red apples. We take our football seriously in Manchester.

CHAPTER TWENTY-FOUR
BORN BLUE (AND NOT FROM LACK OF OXYGEN … MAN U FANS MIGHT WANT TO SKIP THIS BIT)

It's fair to say that my granddad did not exactly approve of my mam's choice of husband. I wasn't there when they were first courting, but I can imagine my granddad getting mad about it.

"I'm not best pleased about this 'r Flo."

"Oh shurrup, Bob."

That's as 'heated' as it ever got with Nana and Granddad. They didn't do 'rows' but Mam and Dad helped out there. So it's not like I was deprived or anything.

And not that I'm sticking up for Granddad, but it was hard for him to deal with Mam marrying a 'foreigner' because he was a real olden days person; born in 1888. Bloomin' eck, by the time I was born, he was on his second Queen. I don't suppose there were many black people in Ancoats when he was a lad. Bless him, he was still struggling with horseless carriages and, God forbid, women riding bicycles which is why I never had one. But that's another story.

Still, every cloud has a silver lining. Dad, being West Indian, didn't give a toss about football. He was a cricket man, which left my football-mad Granddad free to introduce me to the greatest football team in the whole wide world, Manchester City. All you 'Reds' can skip to the next chapter if you want, 'cos I don't care!

Oh yes. I was born Blue, and not through lack of oxygen either. In my nana and granddad's house, sport was taken seriously. Saturday was dedicated to football and wrestling. Although, let's have it right, wrestling was NOT a proper sport; even at my tender age I had sussed out it was a fix. But there was no persuading me nana otherwise. She loved Mick McManus and her weekly fix on *World of Sport*. Still, it must have been a comfort, seeing as she supported Sheffield Wednesday and they played like fairies (me granddad's words not mine).

Mam tells me she actually preferred Man United, but never dared say it when Granddad was alive. (The sound you can hear is him turning in his grave, Mother!) But me? I was and still am City till I bloomin' well die.

It's fair to say that the Granddad I knew and loved had one great love and one great hate in his life. Well, at least the part of his life that concerned me (he was 72 when I was born), and they were Manchester City and Germans. So I imagine he was in a bit of a mither when Bert Trautmann (a German) became City's goalkeeper.

He told me he had attended a demonstration against Mr Trautmann's signing by the club in 1949, just four short years after the war had ended. Nana said he had sulked for weeks.

"The way this bloody world's going 'r Flo, I wouldn't be surprised if Vera Lynn joined the Luftwaffe."

But anyway, Bert worked his magic and played proper good for our beloved Blues and Granddad grudgingly came round ... a bit. By the time Bert retired in 1964 Granddad affectionately referred to him as 'That soddin' German, but he can play'.

Sadly, because of Granddad's age and much more likely the fact he was born in Victorian times when women didn't do nowt if it didn't involve a kitchen, and I was a girl (albeit with a boy's name), he didn't take me to any matches. He did take me to Maine Road though once to meet the players, and I sat on Colin Bell's knee. So bless him for that.

On Saturdays he would go to the bookies. Well, every day he would go to the bookies, but not because he was a gambler. Granddad had been a wages clerk in his working life, and after he had retired he took on another job. I don't know the proper title for what he did but he wrote the 'odds' and stuff like that on a big blackboard.

I used to wait for him outside. To this day, I have never been inside the 'bookies.' I know I can if I want, and loads of women do go in them. But my granddad's words remain with me.

"Only two types of women go in there luv, cleaners or trollops," was his response to my asking if I could go in with him.

"Nana? You go on in the bookies don't you?"

"Yes, luv. I clean there every Tuesday and Thursday."

"And your friend Alice goes there too ... is she a cleaner?"

"No, pet."

"Hmm ... makes sense!"

"Why do you ask?"

"Oh nothing. Just something Granddad said."

Before anyone forwards this to Germaine Greer and she starts bombarding me with abusive tweets or whatever, please remember this was the '60s. Everyone had their place. I'd wait patiently till he came out, always in time for us to get back home and check our pools coupon. It was the highlight of my week in the younger years. He did the pools religiously, and every Saturday me and him would sit at the big table and listen to, or watch the football results; him with his coupon and me with about ten coupons 'cos I was allowed to colour in the squares. You can stick your computer games. This was what fun was all about.

When he'd finished marking his (never won a sausage) he would do a commentary for me to mark mine.

"Right come on 'r Lesley are you ready? Forfar, five, East Fife, four."

I would just break down in gales of laughter. He got me every time.

"An' let's see how your nana's rubbish team have done."

"Oy you 'Bob', you'll be having boiled boots for your tea."

It was Nana's standard response to his teasing. But yet again it never failed to amuse me, and by the time tea was ready I was giggling away and slightly disappointed that Nana hadn't actually boiled any boots.

Because of Granddad I have remained loyal to his (and my) beloved Blues to this day. Through good times and bad, 'cos like Granddad always said, "You can't go through life chopping and changing."

Obviously some mams, no names mentioned, didn't get it, and how they have the cheek to even support that other lot is beyond me. But unlike noses, you can't pick em. So here I am carrying on the Blue tradition as my Grandfather would have wished, whilst his OWN daughter has allowed herself to be dragged over to the other side. I blame George Best and his uncanny resemblance to Englebert Humperdinck!

Some people are just so shallow.

Granddad died when I was almost ten, but I saw him nearly every day of my life during that decade. Not only is he the reason why I support Manchester City, he also taught me about equality. Not 'Man v Woman' equality. Like I said, he was born in the late 1800's and had decidedly old-fashioned views in that area. Not even about black and white equality because again, he was raised in a time when people had the oddest notions about other races. Thank goodness I had Dad to dispel some of them daft ideas or I'd have thought all his family lived in a tree in Africa. The equality Granddad taught me about was concerned with 'class'. He was working class and bloody proud and taught me to be proud too.

"You come from good working class stock 'r Lesley. On your mother's side at least. Never bow to no-one."

"Not even the Queen?"

"Especially not the bloody Queen. What makes her better than you?" *The castles and jewels?*

"She wants to try a day down the pit, never mind flouncing around in pearls and gloves opening bloody this and that."

"You want to try a day down the pit yourself 'r Bob. You worked in a bloody office," piped up me nana from the kitchen. "Stop disrespecting our Queen. People have gone to the tower for less. Don't listen to him, pet, our royal family is the best in the world."

Granddad just did one of his humphs and took out his pipe. "Can I light it for you, Granddad?"

"Course you can, luv," he replied. Good clean fun we had in our pre 'everything is bad for you world'. He whispered in my ear, "Don't ever bow to no one 'r kid."

"I won't Granddad," I whispered back. I've never met the Queen yet, but if I do, I'll shake her hand and that's it.

Don't know where I'd ever bump into her though. We don't exactly move in the same circles round here. Her son is called the Prince of Wales. I wonder if she goes to Rhyl? That's where we go for so-called holidays. It's not a beach if there's no soddin' sand. Just thinking about some of our holidays back then makes me need a rest.

CHAPTER TWENTY-FIVE
WE'RE NOT GOING ON A SUMMER HOLIDAY

When money is tight and you've got a hundred kids, sometimes you can't afford a proper holiday. You have to 'make do and mend'. I don't think me mam ever said that. I probably heard that on telly or something. But it fits this chapter well, so I'm having it.

Here are some fun things to do when it's raining and no one has invented computer games yet (or computers even).

Melt records in hot water to make ash trays, or use an LP to make something bigger. Please note: only use rubbish records and be very aware that your idea of rubbish and your mam's are two very, very different things. Not even the addition of a bunch of grapes can make certain mams appreciate her Jim Reeves *Distant Drums* LP being turned into a decorative, and in my opinion classy, fruit bowl.

Take all the bedding off all the beds and make a den. You will have plenty of material (excuse the pun) to work with. This is the pre-duvet era. So on each bed you have: An eiderdown, two blankets, top sheet, bottom sheet, and in some cases (not mine, honest to God, my eyes are NOT crossed) a rubber sheet. In defence of bed wetters of whom I know absolutely NONE, can I just say, getting up in a cold house to go to the toilet in the middle of the night ain't easy ... I would imagine.

Choose a sibling to pick on. This is a game that never fails to amuse. There are MANY ways to conduct this game, but my favourite is pretending they don't exist, so that when they speak, you just look around the room and say:

"Did anyone hear a noise?" I thought I did, but it must be the ghost of a really ugly kid who NO ONE likes. You sometimes have to pause this game for a bit. Especially if your 'victim' is a 'GRASS' who goes running to her mam (yours too) whingin' and telling tales.

"Mam. 'r Lesley and 'r Karin are pretending I'm not there."

"Oi, you two. Stop picking on your sister, or I'll give you something to pick. Like your ar*es up off of the floor."

"MAM ... she's such a liar. How can we pretend she's not here when she's sat right next to us?" *She is so dead! The tell-tale tit.*

"Well be nice. She's only a baby." *Baby whale more like.*

"OK. C'mon 'r 'manda sit next to me. *Stingray's* coming on. I'm Marina and 'r Karin is Atlanta. You can be a Fish Man. What you cryin' for now?"

"You pinched me. MAAAAAM!"

I definitely am gonna kill her when I get out up off the floor (Mam never makes empty threats) and I'm gonna wipe me bum on her Tippy Tumbles, the evil cow. I did not pinch her. I was straightening out the chair back covers and her big fat arm was in the way.

Invent recipes. This is best done when mams are not in the kitchen. Say for example if the woman next door has just knocked on and said:

"I won't come in. I'm not stopping," which usually means mams will be standing on that doorstep for the next hour or so. This is also the BEST time to ask for permission to be in the kitchen.

"Mam. Can a make a Bu-le le ler in the kit ... room?"

"He did what? You're bloody right to sling him out Jackie. Yes luv, just don't make a mess. I'll be there in a minute. It's his loss pet. You sure you don't want that cuppa?"

"No luv. I've got to get down to the Bendix. Not having anyone saying I threw him out with dirty shirts." Grown-ups are funny people, and I don't mean ha, ha.

Anyway, new recipes. Let's see what's in the cupboard. Ah Bread. Can't have a butty without bread. Brown sauce, salad cream, salt, pepper. OK now let's see what's on the windowsill (the fridge of the olden days). Nowt! What is it me granddad says about Nana?

"She can make a feast from a famine can my Flo." (Mam definitely didn't inherit THAT talent.)

Gawd! Doesn't pepper travel? I only gave it a little sprinkle. Just to accentuate the sauce on my brown sauce butty an' it's gone everywhere. When 'r 'manda stops sneezing I'll make her clean it up.

"What the bloody hell is going on in here? Who said you could come in here? Don't I have enough to do without having to constantly clean up after you lot? Do you want to put me in an early grave?"

For God's sake, Woman, give me a chance to answer one question before you start on the next, and how do you do that? Just appear out of nowhere? Last time I looked, you and Jackie were comparing 'spells'.

"I don't know Mam. I just came in the kitchen and saw 'r 'manda making a mess."

"Oh yes? Really?" (I don't think she believes me ... gulp!)

"Bedroom, NOW! And stop blaming the baby for everything. She can't even walk without her walker. So you tell me, how did she reach that top cupboard? And before you LIE just remember I've got the belt in my hand."

"Er, I was lifting her up to get the gripe water 'cos she said her tummy was hurting and she just grabbed everything. Ouch Mam that hurt!"

"It was meant to. You're gonna end up in Strangeways you!"

Anyway, like I said, it's raining! so we can't play out. What's a kid or several to do? Well, when your mam has insisted you watch every Judy Garland/Mickey Rooney film that comes on the telly there's only one option. Let's put on a show! Now, Mam was as house-proud as you could be with the Von Trapp kids in permanent residence, and worked hard to maintain cleanliness.

"If a single drop falls on my kitchen floor you'll know about it. Now sit down, shut up and enjoy your dinner."

"What is it with YOU and forks? Lean over the soddin' plate or I'll give you a spoon, like a baby. There's more rice on this floor than in China." (What an exaggerator and just a tad racist ... by 1980's PC standards ... but, hey, this was the '60s.)

In later years though:

"How can it be racist to call your dad coloured? That's what he is. You see that coffee table there? That's black! And mixed-race? What nonsense is that, me and your dad are both from the human race. You're half-caste. Now shut it!"

"Well that fridge is white and it's not like you and it could be twins." (All it took to bring out the 'rebel' in me was one episode of *Roots*. Oh and being 25 helped, nearly!)

"I should have let them put you in a home!"

Anyway, back to the swinging '60s and Mam's quest to be on the cover of *Perfect Homes*. (By swinging I mean the kind you do in the park.)

"WHO'S been sat on this chair?" (It's a CHAIR, that's its purpose.) "I know it's you Madam." She's looking at me again. It's possible she has a wandering eye, and I'm being unfair in my feeling of persecution, but? "I can see the imprint of your knees in my velvet cushion cover. They cost a fortune. SIT PROPERLY or don't sit at all."

Great choice. Deportment lessons or a lifetime of standing, anyway I've got your knees. That's what you always tell people.

"If it wasn't for the knees, I'd swear she wasn't mine. She's HIM from top to toe, excluding the knee area. Every time I try to forget him, up she pops with THAT face." I'm gonna French knit a balaclava and wear it back to front. Will that help?

"We're bored Mam and there's nowt to do. Can we go to Blackpool? It is the summer holidays and we haven't even been anywhere yet."

"Have you got Blackpool money?" Why does she ask ridiculous questions? I'm nine and apparently I don't even qualify for family allowance. "And why are you lying? I took you to Heaton Park last week."

"That's not a holiday. Heaton Park is round here. Can't we go somewhere on a Sharra and stay in a caravan?"

"Not this year. The only person in this house who's getting a holiday this year is your dad." She means Strangeways and she sent him for not paying the maintenance for us. Me mam doesn't just make threats. She makes promises and keeps them.

"This 'ere piece of paper is a legal separation mate, an' it says on here you've got to support me and your kids. If you're not here on Friday morning with my shopping money, I'll be seeing you in court."

Nana brought our shopping that Friday and the week after, the man in a suit (with a case an' all, but he was no Richard Bradford) came. (See Chapter 2.)

"I'll take you all to Nana's next week and she'll take you for a walk in the symmetry."

"Yeah but we're bored now and it's raining. What can we do NOW?"

"Bleedin' 'ell, you of all people weren't at the back of the queue when they were giving out imaginations. Think of something and get out of my sight or I'll give you a sore backside and you can play with that." I'm GONE.

It's the SHOW option then. I'll be the director. Where did I put my megaphone, jodhpurs and whip? Oh that's right I don't have any. I'll have to make do and mend. That's the bonus with a good Northern saying. You get to use it twice in one chapter, talk about a bargain. Cheap at half the price (that's another one).

"Karin, Amanda, Melissa, come here. We're gonna do a show for Mam. Get 'r Wayne too, he can be a prop."

"I'm colouring in. I don't want to do a show," says Karin. I'll colour her a black eye in a minute.

"Mam says you have to."

"I'm gonna ask her."

"NO don't do that. She also said the next person to go in the kitchen is getting a tanned arse." She falls for it - sounds like typical Mam.

We all sit on the bed, some of us more grudgingly than others, and think of what song to do.

"Should we do *High Hopes* by Frank Sinatra?" suggests Amanda.

"Frank Sinatra?" Mam's Mancunian soprano is starting to come out in me. "What century are you from? We need to do something modern ... I know, *Summer Holiday* by Cliff Richard!" I love Cliff Richard (third, after Dad and Troy Tempest). None of the others do. But then again they're all idiots, and this isn't a democracy. I'm the eldest and biggest, although Melissa is catching up fast; it's all them extra scoops. What I say goes. Three sets of shoulders sink. I swear one of 'em just tutted. If I find out who it is ...

"What's 'r Wayne gonna be?"

"A beach ball. We can boot him up and down the bedroom floor whilst we're singing."

"Mam'll go mad."

"I'm only joking. We'll throw that mustard-coloured blanket on him. Pretend he's a sandcastle." I'll kick it at the end. Everyone loves to kick a sandcastle. Got to keep it authentic. Mam will understand. On second thoughts ...

We begin rehearsals. Two hours of hard work later (that clock must be slow) and we're ready.

We've made a stage by hanging up two sheets, one on the wardrobe and one on the top of the window. I've had to make a little teeny hole in the one on the window sill, so it can attach to the nail holding the net wire up. The one on the wardrobe is easy. We just trap it in the door. We join 'em in the middle with a peg and Mam's big sweeping brush. *Just as an aside, don't teeny weeny holes spread? By the time we took the sheet down you could climb through the hole. We've got another couple of days till she changes the bedding. Plenty of time to think of an excuse.*

"Mam. Are you coming? We're ready now."

"Yes. Just give me a minute. I'm washing the pots." That'll be a Mancunian Mam minute. We'd better settle down this could take a while. Might as well read

War and Peace whilst we're waiting ... can probably fit in *Gone with the Wind* too.

Eventually she gets there and takes her seat. We've borrowed three of the kitchen chairs to make it look more theatrey. She gets up from her seat to take the blanket off Wayne.

"Bloody 'ell, me son's suffocating under there." What a drama queen. It's her that should be on the stage. I stick 'r 'manda's Tippy Tumbles under the blanket instead. I need authenticity to perform. I'm the Marlon Brando of Moston, and it'll be almost as much fun to kick that instead. Anyway the batteries have run out and no one ever replaces a battery in our house so I don't even see the point of the stupid doll. They should rename it Tippy Tumbles For a Bit.

We only know the first verse of *Summer Holiday*. So we sing it ten times. Got to give the audience its money's worth. Mam is so into the music, she seems to be in a world of her own. We finish singing. I kick the bucket and we all bow.

Mam starts clapping. "That was ... wonderful. Now clean this room. I'm gonna put your tea out."

Clean the room? I'm a star. I'm not cleaning no room. "OK, Mam."

"Right you lot, get this bedroom tidied up or I'm gonna batter ya." They know I'm not messing. I've got my Hollywood face on, and a pair of clackers in my hand.

Two hours later ...

"Mam I'm bored."

"Oh, for God's sake. Nana's coming tomorrow. You can go back with her for a bit." Hurrah!

CHAPTER TWENTY-SIX
IT'S LIKE BEING AN ONLY CHILD (I WISH!)

"It's your turn to stay at Nana and Granddad's this weekend."

Apart from "It's your Birthday/Easter/Christmas next week," these were the best words that ever came out of me mam's mouth. I'm not including the wisdom and life guidancey type stuff so don't be sulking, Lady!

A weekend at Nana and Granddad's meant a weekend of being treated like a Queen. The only kid and two old people who thought the sun shone out of your backside. What could be better?

I sat there with me coat on and me pyjamas rolled up under me arm from the moment I knew I was going.

Dad had a car, but Nana always came for us on the bus. I loved going on the bus. She'd get to ours just after dinner (one o'clockish for the posh readers). She and Mam would have a cup of tea and a natter in the kitchen. Me Nana would say "I told you so" a lot and Mam would be saying "Well this time I've had enough." (Probably been eating chocolates again.) Sometimes she'd come to the kitchen door at the exact moment I was walking past, so it looked like I'd been standing there all the time, *how unfair is life*, do that look where she tuts and looks at the ceiling, looks back down and sees dog poo, then shuts the door. Those were the times I really felt sorry for Dad. They were destroying him in there, and when he came in, boosted by Nana's considered opinion that "You're right 'r Joyce," she would proper start on him. But at the same time I didn't care (sorry Dad, kids are selfish sometimes) 'cos I was going to Nana's. So they could entertain the others with their witty banter.

"She's just a friend."

"Just a FRIEND?" *It's back! Mancunian soprano.* "If that's how you behave with a 'friend,' God help the woman in the paper shop."

Makes no sense when she's mad does me mam. Ninety-nine per cent of the time I reckon she's mad about something!

Just got to wait for Nana now. It's Friday, so no worries about having to wait till the wrestling is done. The only man I reckon she'd leave Granddad for is Mick McManus ... Oh, and one of the Bachelors ... or all three, and that Val Doonican, too. Bloomin' eck, Granddad is on dodgy ground here. Me nana's a floozy!

She's straightening her girdle. We'll be off soon.

"C'mon 'r Lesley, the bus'll be here soon, and we've a better chance of getting it if we're actually stood at a bus stop."

She laughs. I do too, but not at that joke; at the looks of pure jealousy on me sisters' faces. I give them my customary goodbye of 'tongue sticking out' and shoulder wobbling.

"One of us is getting a cake tomorrow and I'll give you a clue. It's none of you lot. BYE!"

I leave them all in a state of fumingness and grab me nana's hand. We're off.

Even the familiar journey is exciting. Down two flights of stairs. Up to the top end of Thornton Street North, and onto Collyhurst Street. I may well turn out to have an addictive personality when I'm older, because there's loads of railings and I'm shaking 'cos I haven't got a stick.

Under the railway bridge, which I pretend is the Tunnel of Love at Blackpool. Mam says:

"No you're not going on the Tunnel of Love. You're too young for that nonsense."

Round the corner to the bus stop on Oldham Road. Although to me it's the other big road, the one that doesn't go to the CIS (Rochdale Road; both these roads lead to places where people talk funny). Now, I'll play the guess which bus will come first game, whilst Nana tells some lady we've never ever met before about her varicose veins and how me dad isn't from round these parts.

"We were heartbroken when she met HIM. Our only child with one of THEM. Still, what can you do? They're me grandkids, me flesh and blood and I love 'em. If they ask any questions I just tell 'em God left your dad in the oven too long."

I 'tut' and carry on swinging round the bus stop. Dad's been teaching me about my history on his side for as long as I can remember. Nana's daft, but I love her.

Here comes the bus. Oh good, it's the 88. That one goes past the haunted house of horrors where people with the mange and hideous diseases that give them two heads live, otherwise known as Monsall.

It was actually a tropical diseases hospital I found out later in life. But you know how kids are.

I knew we were getting close when the bus went past the playhouse on Kenyon Lane, then past me mam's old school Lily Lane. It's dead hard to believe mam went to school but I had it under good authority (me nana) that she did, and Mam herself had told me. But unlike me, Mam had hated school. She told me that once she had tried to escape and had got impaled on the railings. It left a big scar on her knee. She'd tried to tell me once she got it "Booting a naughty kid to the moon and back," but Nana confirmed the railing story.

Soon we were at the corner of Kenyon Lane and Moston Lane, the proper Moston. There was the Ben Brierley, me nana's pub. Don't get me wrong, she didn't spend her evenings propping up the bar, a Senior Service in one hand and a half of milk stout in the other. She did that at home.

In later years the doctor asked her to cut down on her cigs.

"Why don't you try something a bit milder, Mrs Holden. You need to take better care of yourself." So she changed to Capstan Full Strength and did a push up every three drags.

Now, Nana, as I've already mentioned, was the cleaner. I reckoned she loved her job because she was always happy. At least she said she was.

"Right 'r Bob I'm off to the 'Ben'. They had a visiting darts team from Salford in last night and a platter of sardine sandwiches. Those toilets'll be fun." For non Mancs, a sandwich is a butty. Me nana was from Sheffield. They talk the same but different.

I decide to play out for a bit. I call for my Moston mates, Julie and Suzanne.

Julie lives a few doors down from Nana. Her dad has a camera. I don't know anyone else in real life who has a camera. He took a good few pictures of me which nowadays I'm really grateful for. Photographs were expensive in them days and you usually had to go into town to a studio if you wanted a photo taken. My favourite is one where I'm folding my arms and sulking. Not 'cos I'm having my picture taken but 'cos Dad had dressed me that morning before dropping me off at Nana's. Mam was in hospital having her leg off (only joking, she was having another kid) and he's put 'r Karin's cardigan on me. The wrists were round my elbows. I looked a right tit. Her house is a bit posher than Nana's too. They've got a proper bathroom and an inside toilet. But I still love Nana's house more.

We go round the corner to Hinde Street to call for Suzanne. Her mam and dad are hippies. They are really young and trendy but still like a proper mam and dad too, with rules.

"Where are you'se going?"

(Spain!) "Just across the road. We're gonna play two-ball."

147

"OK Don't go anywhere else without letting us know."

Don't parents fret? The wall we're gonna play two-ball on is right opposite their house.

We play two-ball for ages:

Pontius Pilate King of the Jews.

Bought his wife a pair of shoes,

When the shoes began to wear,

Pontius Pilate bought a bear.

(Or summat like that.)

With each round, the method of throwing the ball got progressively harder: Underarm, overarm, back to front, etc, etc. Until one person was left the winner. The prize was the satisfaction of winning.

When we were all played out, or hungry, we all went to our respective homes. See you next time girls, and that's how it went in my younger years. No complicated friendships amongst young kids. If you were about, you played out together. If you didn't see each other for a few months, so what? You just picked up where you left off.

Nana was usually home by the time I come in, and I just knew I was getting a cake for after my tea. If it was a Saturday I would have an egg custard 'cos Nana ALWAYS made trifle for Sunday. I was allowed to help, too. She would pour the boiling water on, but I was allowed to break up the jelly cubes (and eat one or two) and stir them till they melted. When I got a bit bigger I was allowed to carry the bowl into the front room to set on the window sill. No central heating back then. The front room was always cold ... even in summer. Perfect for jelly setting.

After tea and the pools with Granddad, I would get my nightie on and settle down for an evening of telly with my lovely grandparents. At bedtime, Granddad would tell me stories about the war till I fell asleep. How I didn't have nightmares, I'll never know. Some of his tales, especially the ones about shell shock, were slightly scary.

The next day it would be a lovely Sunday dinner and singing something simple on the radio. If it was a school day the next day, Nana would take me home. The bus ride home was never as fun as the one TO Moston. Each landmark disappearing till we reached the railway junction box at the top of our street and it was time to get off.

Back to chaos and all those kids. I suppose I did miss them ... and Mam and Dad too, but it was nice to be an only child once in a while.

CHAPTER TWENTY-SEVEN
HOW DID I GET HERE? (NOT THE CHAPTER, I MEAN, HOW DID I GET HERE?)

So, how did I come to be blessed to be a Mancunian? Well it wasn't easy. Me mam herself was half foreign. Granddad was a proper Manc born in Ancoats. A Robert 'Bob' from a traceable line of six Robert 'Bob's' originating in Middlewich, Cheshire and ending up in Moston. Apart from France and Italy in the war (the first one!) the furthest he had gone was Blackpool in wakes week. I wasn't best pleased when I found out he'd been all these places without me, but I let him off seeing as it was about 100 years before I was born. In my lifetime, he never got further than Moston Lane. But bless him, he did walk with a stick. He got injured fighting for his country. His wife, who I knew as Nana, and who me mam called Mam, was slightly more exotic.

It was rumoured that her father was a Russian-Jewish immigrant who had escaped the pogroms in Russia at the turn of the century and had settled in Sheffield. While there he became a metal worker and met and married Nana's mam, a local girl called Annie.

I don't know why I said "rumoured" 'cos to be honest it was only ever mentioned in the immediate family. We weren't the Astors or anything. But it was one of those family 'things' we all have, where you only kind of talk about it.

"So where was your mam and dad from Nana?"

"Well, my Mother came from Woodhouses. But my Father came ..."

"There's no need to go into too much detail, Mam. She's only a kid."

God, it's like you don't want me to learn anything. You want thick kids.

"Go on Nana, tell me."

I can push it a bit. Nana always sticks up for me, and it's dead funny when she tells me mam off.

"He was from Russia, and his family were Jewish."

WOW! *What does that mean ... Jewish?* But Russia, I knew that. I'd seen them on the telly. They always wore fur hats and talked English, but with a funny accent.

They were all spies, I think. OMG, I'm Mata Hari. Granddad had told me about her. I'm sure he said she was Russian. I'd thought he meant fast, but decided against asking and had kept me mouth shut, 'cos when he went off on a tangent you were in danger of getting piles. Which is what happens when you're stuck in one place too long, listening to his never-ending tales.

A few days later I watched *Carve Her Name with Pride* and *The Diary of Anne Frank*. You missed the first ten minutes of Anne Frank 'cos it was on the other channel. Not ANOTHER, that's right OTHER. We only had two, then three when BBC2 started, and that's how it remained till I grew up. So consequently, we'd watch owt. Anyway, both were very good films, and to a kid with my dramatic bent, watching stuff like this led to my spending the rest of the weekend planning my future job as resistance fighter. Every day I prayed for a war in my lifetime. Every grown-up I knew was always saying how great things were during the war. The lucky sods even had powered egg. Astronauts had powdered eggs ... wow! We had to make do with boring real ones. I hated the brown ones. They were the ones that were good for you. I liked my eggshell like I liked my bread - white.

If I was impressed by the thought of Russian blood, by the time I'd watched *The Diary of Anne Frank* I was apoplectic with delight. Not at the thought of what happened, but at the romance of it all. I was only about eight by this time so it was a few more years before I realised the absolute horror of what the Jews went through during World War II. To me it meant I was related to Moses (had seen *The Ten Commandments* too). Maybe the tea-towel incident (see Chapter 3) wasn't the nun coming out in me. Maybe it was my biblical side. Oh Lord, pass me a bagel. I was a Chosen One.

So, the half of me that came from Mam was pretty exotic, even if the exoticism had been somewhat lost somewhere between the Russian steppes, Sheffield and Ancoats via Moston and Collyhurst.

As for Dad, well that was another story of trials and tribulations. Well it was by the time I'd finished.

Dad was a proper foreigner. Not even born here. He came from Barbados. Nowadays everyone knows where Barbados is, thanks to Typically Tropical's number one hit from 1975, oh yeah and Rihanna, but back then no one I ever knew had a clue where it was.

Dad was a bit of a mix too. His maternal grandmother was a Native American from the Apache tribe and his dad was an African-American who had come to Barbados as a young man, where he had made his fortune in real estate and had been a major player on the political scene. He was instrumental in the battle to achieve independence for Barbados, which happened in 1966. The Queen didn't seem to have a problem with this as the next year he came to London and she gave him a medal called a CBE.

Because of this wonderful mix of African, Indian, Russian Jew and native

English, some people had trouble working out what me and my siblings were (like it was their business anyhow), and like many bigots they got it wrong.

"Mam, someone just called me a Paki."

"Well get back out there and say: 'I'm not a Paki I'm a Nigger and proud!'"

Never bow to no-one. That's how I was raised. Be proud of what you are and don't let a horrible name define you. If it's said to you with hatred you just embrace it and turn it around with pride. So if anyone ever said a racial slur, I'd just reply: "Yes I am a Nigger/wog/coon and can I just congratulate you on your wonderful powers of deduction." The look of confusion on their faces was hysterical.

On the face of it, that me and my siblings ever existed at all was a marvellous feat. First of all my dad had to exasperate his own dad with his naughty ways to the point where Granddad had him shipped over here. The story is he got one or two ladies in the family way (at the SAME time!) and Granddad was just getting into his political stride and could do without the embarrassment, so he sent him over here to go to University. He was meant to be going to London, but for reasons unknown aka 'fate' he ended up in Manchester. Then Mam had to lie to her parents and the door staff at the Ritz in town. She was only 17, and had told her mam and dad that she and her friend Bessie were going to learn how to type at evening classes. *And she wondered where I got MY sly ways from?*

Anyway that's how these two people, born 3,500 miles apart, both ended up in the Ritz on a Friday night. Six years later God blessed them with me. He obviously meant me to be a Manc. Can't get better than that.

* * *

I love being British, but equally I love my other bits too. We've got everything in my family: black, white, Christian, Muslim, Jew. We can't hate anyone except southerners. Only joking, we don't hate 'em at all. Just can't stand 'em and their faffy ways. Whenever I go 'darn sarf' (they talk funny too), I always meet some joker who says, "Hey oop luv, that big thing in the sky is called the sun," OR "You're from Manchester? Where's your brolly?"

I'm from the best city in the world. The 'dark satanic mills' have all but gone. The spirit that got us through the hardships of the olden days remains. And on top of that we've got the best football team in the world and Manchester United, too.

CHAPTER TWENTY-EIGHT
ROAST POTATOES AND THE NIT COMB? IT MUST BE SUNDAY

How to tell what day it is, when you're six-and-a-half:

Monday: Anything not nailed down gets washed and mangled. Kitchen gets bottomed.

Tuesday: Nothing on telly. Ornaments get washed. Kitchen gets bottomed.

Wednesday: Half-day closing. That's the day Mam says she'll take you to Woolworths if you hang on a bit.

"Oh is that the time? Sorry luv we won't get there before they shut."

"OMG nip downstairs and get us a loaf/milk/fags or there'll be no toast/cup of tea/hope for you lot if I don't have me cigs." Kitchen gets bottomed.

Thursday: Pay day. Big shop at the Spar. Chippy tea. *Top of the Pops.* Kitchen ... (you get the drift).

Friday: Stay up late till at least the middle of the night - 8 o'clock. We were idiots!

Saturday: No school. Playing out, Wrestling on telly. Go home, Nana!

Sunday: Roast potatoes and the nit comb.

Nowadays you can have roast potatoes whenever you want. But when I was a kid, I think it was against the law to have them any other day but Sunday.

"You want roast potatoes? It's soddin' Wednesday! I'm not one of the great train robbers. I've not got money for roast potatoes. You're having chips or nowt!"

Does she realise what she just said? A chip IS ... oh never mind. She won't listen anyway, and she's edging towards the belt as we speak. Don't want her to reach the point of no return, which is also the point of absolutely ridiculous questions.

"Do you really want me to get that belt?"

Who mentioned anything about a belt? I certainly didn't.

"Have I not warned you about giving me cheek?"

You never give a warning. One minute you're shouting, next minute you're belting.

"Do you want something to cry for?"

No thanks, I've already found something.

And the classic:

"If you make me come back in this room, you'll know about it."

Not technically a question, but it always puzzled me.

So chips it is then. Homemade ones, too, the chippy never opens on a Wednesday. Don't fret dear reader, chips ain't stew. She does lovely chips. Oh God, what are them tinned tomatoes doing there?

"What else are we having Mam?"

"Fried egg and tinned tomatoes. "

I HATE tinned tomatoes. Tinned tomatoes are like great big blobs of watery blood that taste like great big blobs of watery blood.

"I don't like tinned tomatoes, can I just have egg?" Sounds like a reasonable request to me.

"If you think I'm gonna start serving up different meals to you lot you've got another think coming." (What the eck does that mean?) "It's not a bloody café, you'll have the same as everyone else. I blame your dad, taking you to London. Tea at the Ritz at your age?"

Oh, somebody call the police. How dare he take his child for a scone?

And thus began the saga that was to be known by future generations as, The Battle of the Tinned Tomatoes.

I was seven she was 21, and remained 21 till I found her birth certificate. *Yep, rooting again.*

We sat facing each other across the Formica table, which was always covered in a checked tablecloth. I used to stare at the checks on it until my eyes went funny. She moved the sauce bottle. Not only was it blocking her view, she wanted to lean in closer. There we were, nose to nose.

"You will eat that tinned tomato ... You will not leave this table till that tinned tomato is eaten. You will stay here all night if you have to, until the tinned tomato has gone. And don't blame me if the monsters get you. It's a TOMATO, it's good for you. Eat the BLOODY TOMATO."

She leaves. I look at the tomato. I look at the floor. She's hidden the bin! I look all around, then I look at the ceiling. I look down. I look at the ceiling again. I look at the tomato. I look back at the ceiling ...

A short while later, she returns.

"There you go. See! You're not dead! How hard was it, eating a tomato? You've got vitamins inside you now. Go on, go outside and find your sisters, we'll have chippy for tea."

THREE DAYS LATER!

I'm still too traumatised to share my experience of what followed. You'll have to make do with an extract from the official transcript.

The Place: Kitchen of ** Thornton St North, Collyhurst.

Those present: Myself, my mother by birth, three or four other kids and next door's dog.

Time of incident: Before *Magic Roundabout* but after *Trumpton*.

Details of incident: An explosive device, later identified as a 'tinned tomato' (untinned by the way), inexplicably landed on the Formica table resulting in unsightly stains on blouse of Mother, and a beige Labrador that has the appearance of having been stabbed multiple times.

Punishment: After a short dance round the Formica table by both parties, a good hiding was given, to be followed by a lifetime of recrimination.

But, back to the Sunday routine, beloved of the Mancunian family. For some of us the first act of the day was going to church. Mam has always believed in God, but was never particularly church-going. So mostly she sent us on her behalf (how crafty is that?) and let me tell you, it was nowt like *Joan of Arc* or *The Sound of Music*. Mostly, it was proper boring.

Then back home to the smell of Sunday dinner. Hmmm, something smells nice. Dad must be cooking. We shall eat like Kings and Queens today, and if we don't bugger it up with greediness, there'll be enough left over to save us from Mam's stew for another day or two.

Sunday is also music day. I'm in charge of the radiogram, but the other kids all get to pick a record each. It's not fair, they're idiots!

"Mam, will you tell 'r Karin? She keeps putting everything on '78 speed, so Cliff Richard sounds like Pinky and Perky, an 'Manda only wants to play Frank Sinatra. I hate YOUR kids. They're ruining my life."

"Oh shurrup ya miserable git." *Charming!* "Put some Englebert on."

"NO!" We all pipe up in unison. At least we agree on something. Dad comes in and takes over. Sam Cooke blasts out of the speakers. We all take turns to dance with him. I stand on his feet whilst he twirls me around the room. When I grow up, I'm going to marry me dad. Then Mother interrupts, "Right 'r Lesley, come and help me set the table."

I feel like a downstairs member of the *Upstairs, Downstairs* cast. I swear she only had me for the help.

"Can I sit next to Dad?" Or anywhere that's far away from you?

"You'll sit where I put you. What's wrong with your face?"

"Nowt." Phew, she almost nearly caught me doing the 'look' (tongue out, head wobbling side to side).

"Can I have a leg?"

"You had one last week. "

"No I didn't. "

"Yes you bloody well did. I've marked it down in me book."

She's not an Enid Blyton or owt like that. She writes down stuff in a little red notebook she bought from the post office. Usually accompanied by cries of "I've got more soddin' week than money!" or "You lot cost a bloody fortune, and I don't get a PENNY family allowance for you!" She means me. It's a bugger being the eldest.

"So who's having the leg then?" It's not a one-legged chicken. Dad always has a leg, and we take it in turns, which works out to a leg every six months or so. She should stop having kids or start serving octopus. Not that I'd eat any of that foreign muck.

"It's 'r Karin's turn."

"Oh." I paused to think for a moment. "Where's she sitting?"

"There. Where you've put the plate with the blue edge."

We only get the posh matching stuff out if someone special comes. To date, no one special has come. The posh plates live in a display cabinet in the living room.

She turns away to slice up her homemade gravy. I stick my finger up my nose and wipe it on Karin's plate. Enjoy that!

"Go and call your dad and the others. Dinner's ready."

"Dad, Mam says to come for your dinner and 'Manda, Mam says you're too fat so you can't have anything."

"I heard that!" God! That woman's got magic ears.

"I was only joking!"

"I'll 'joke' you into next week madam, if you don't watch that mouth."

I'm tempted to look in the mirror and say, "I'm watching, it ain't doing much." But I'm 'chicken', and I want some chicken.

Dad sits at the top of the table and carves. Mam serves the veg.

"I don't want cabbage, thank you." I MUST get points for politeness.

"No cabbage, NO chicken." Tut.

"Just a bit, then." She piles a mound of it on my plate; I'm sure she doesn't like me.

Mind you, I don't think she likes any of us. The faces on me sisters soon drop when their plates are piled high with it too. Next, it's the roast potatoes. Lovely, and Dad tops it off with roast chicken.

"Does anybody want gravy?"

"NO," we all cry in perfect unison. We're like a choir except some of us can't carry a tune to save our life. No names mentioned ... Karin, Amanda and Melissa.

I'm dead musical. But I've mentioned that in Chapter 25.

We tuck in. Mam and Dad chat away. Well, Mam chats, Dad just says "Yes Joyce, no Joyce. I told you, she's a friend of my friend's."

"You enjoying that leg 'r Karin?" I'll tell her about my snot on her plate when she's finished and Mam's not around.

I wait till we've all sat down to watch the Sunday afternoon film. Mam's tidying up the records and mumbling on about Frankie Vaughan.

"If this scratch doesn't come out of my *Give Me The Moonlight*, you're all going to bed early."

I whisper in me sister's ear.

"You ate my snot, 'cos I wiped it on your plate." Well, if looks could kill. Ha, ha, ha the face on her.

"Maaaaaaammmm!"

Shurrup, you daft cow.

"'r Lesley said summat rude."

Honest to God. Sisters! No soddin' loyalty. I know what this means. The belt! Because me mam went through a 'children should be seen and not heard' phase, which lasted for about, the first 18 years of my childhood, I quickly learned to convey my thoughts and feelings via facial expressions. Unfortunately, I was a butty short of a picnic in Queens Park when it came to not getting caught, pulling a face!

"What've you just done?" Are you deaf? Didn't little Miss Gobshite here shout it out loud enough?

"Nowt, Mam. Honest."

"What's 'r Karin going on about then?"

"Nowt. I was just telling her she can play with my Cinderella high heels."

"Oooh, can I?"

"If you don't tell Mam what I've did to your plate, you can," I hiss. A bit of bribery works wonders.

Mam's suspicious, though.

"What's going on?"

"NUFFINK. God Mam why don't you believe me?"

"Oh let me count the ways. "

What a joker. She goes back to waffling on about her precious records. I stick my tongue out at her, quickly. Just not quickly enough.

"Don't you look at me with THAT face, Madam!"

"It's the only face I've got, Missus!" I said, Mam, really.

"Well when I'm telling you that Frankie Vaughan was a heartthrob, I don't want to turn around and see YOU trying to look at the inside of your head, whilst your tongue is heading in the direction of your chin!"

"I WASN'T! I had an itchy ... . er, ITCH."

"Are you giving me cheek?"

"No! I'm answering your question."

"Are you TALKING BACK to me?"

"NOOOOO! I'm answering your first question! About Frankie Fingy." And I don't even know what a 'heartthrob' is. All I know is I do not like that thing he does with his leg when he sings *Give Me The Moonlight*. And honest to gor! (gurgling noise ... fingers crossed, eyes crossed ... toes trying), "Mam. I WASN'T pulling a face!"

She believes me, she believes me not ...

She's giving me that, 'I've given birth to a 'Gobshite' but one of us is going to have to give in, and it int me' look.

I'm giving her the 'and it i'n't me, either' look back!

"The ONE thing I won't tolerate from a KID, is CHEEK. GET TO YOUR ROOM. NOW!"

"Why do people say 'cheek'? What do they mean? Do they mean that the cheek on our faces is naughty? Can mams see a special sign on our cheeks?"

"Stop asking BLOODY questions all the bloody time. I'm getting bloody sick of it." *Well pardon me for wanting to expand my knowledge.*

"I'm gonna ask Dad. Dad knows loads of stuff. You only know about Englebert Humpledinkle and babies."

OUCH! That hurt.

In my opinion, what I really think about corporal punishment is: When you get the 'belt', the actual 'getting' of the belt should be punishment in itself.

Why do I have to go to my room as well? That's like a double punishment. Who has fun in a bedroom? I am six-and-a-half, (nowt in here but beds and candlewicks).

I can hear my sisters in the living room. They're watching *Abbot and Costello Meet the Mummy*, and laughing at me. The cows! I'm gonna kill 'em when they come to bed! Might as well justify the punishment, all this for pulling one little face, and a teensy bit of snot on a plate!

There's a mark on the back of me leg from the belt. It's not very big though, 'tut'. I know, I'll give meself a rope burn. Where's that skipping rope? Ouch! That'll make her feel guilty.

(Big sigh.) I'm proper fed up now. I've blown me nose on all me sister's nighties, till me snot ran out. Amanda laughed the loudest, so I've wiped me bum on her 'Tiny Tears'. Can't wait to tell her after she's given the doll its good-night kiss and cuddle. I've been in here for ages. The film's nearly finished.

I see my bedroom door start to open. I put on my 'I'm sorry but in no way am I admitting I was wrong' face.

Me mam comes in the room - without knocking - what a cheek. But then again it's the '60s ... we had parents with absolute power.

"Let me see ya. Hmm, funny how two strokes of the 'belt' gives you a rope burn. Is that skin on 'r Karin's skipping rope?"

I do my best to look mortified she should even think that! It mustn't have worked 'cos she's laughing at me.

"C'mon. I'm putting the tea out. Ham butties and Angel Delight. Then it's big bath time."

God. Pleasure and pain in one sentence.

Ham butties. Oh what luxury. On thick white bread, with butter and English mustard, which I didn't really like but felt obliged to have.

Angel Delight. Butterscotch flavour. The absolute poshest desert ever, till Arctic Roll came out. Nowadays it's Viennetta. Me mam being a tight cow, however, wouldn't put it in the long-stemmed glasses, like they did on the advert. But it still tasted lovely, even if it was served in a Pyrex cereal bowl.

So that's the pleasure, along with something good on the telly. But what about the 'pain'?

That comes in the form of big bath time and a poison tasting session.

This is not a midweek jump in with your sister splash-about 'cos neither of you listened when she said:

"I'm warning you. Stay away from that coalhole."

This is the bath time that hurts, where she scrubs your ears out and washes your hair and believe you me, there was no such thing as 'No More Tears' shampoo in those days. She used Vosene or Loxene. Both were guaranteed to strip your hair of everything, even hair, but funnily enough, NOT nits.

Somewhere in the handbook for '60s parents is a section dedicated to appropriate torture for kids. I would imagine the one that hurts the most was the dreaded nit comb.

Now, I'm not going to lie. I did get nits once or twice as a child. It can't be helped. I was always round other kids, whether at school or at home. Anyone from round here who tells you they never had nits is either a liar or spent the first 15 years of their life as bald as the kid in Hans Christian Anderson. The shaven head look was not as popular as it is today. In fact, when I was a kid, anyone who had a shaved head and wasn't Yul Brynner probably had impetigo or nits. Or, in the case of Jackie's son, both.

"Right, who's first?" she says, casting her evil eye over the four of us. We're all standing shivering and hanging on to the fireguard. Bloody cold in those days with no central heating. I don't even know why she asks. She's gonna choose me first anyway, as usual.

"Come on 'r Lesley, you first."

Oh, the delights of being the eldest. Still, once it's over I can sit back and relax, and laugh at the others.

The torture begins. First, it's the rubdown with her finest quality sandpaper towels.

"Ow Mam, you're hurting!"

"Try walking round with chafed thighs. Then you'll know pain."

I can't breathe. She's covered me from me neck to me toes in talc. It looks like a snowstorm in here. She starts combing my hair.

"What do you do to get lugs like this? Every bloody morning I brush it, and every bloody night you've got lugs. You'll have to sit down, I can't reach the top of your head Miss Lanky Drawers."

She pulls the nit comb from my scalp to the end of my hair and examines it after each pull.

"Nope. Can't see any nit eggs." Bet there's enough skin off me scalp though. Me head is stinging. After what seems like an eternity she plaits it into two pigtails. Thank God that's over. But worse is to come.

"Right, medicine time."

"I'm not sick."

"And do you know WHY you're not sick? 'Cos prevention is better than cure. Now get this down ya and you can sit down and watch telly for a bit."

She shovels a spoonful of some horrible black treacle stuff down my throat. The spoon hits the back of my mouth and makes me gag.

"Don't you dare. Right, a bit of castor oil now and you're done."

At least the black stuff is sweet. Castor oil is mingin. But I swallow and suffer. If I bring it up I'm only gonna have to have another one.

Dressing gown and slippers, and I'm done. Time to settle down and laugh at them lot, watch telly for a bit, then some cocoa and toast and off to bed, with lovely clean bedding. Bless me mam. Sunday was never a day of rest for her. But despite the nit comb and horrible medications, I loved it.

CHAPTER TWENTY-NINE
WAIT AND SEE!

I hope you can surmise from the previous chapters that all-in-all I had a wonderful childhood. Not rich, certainly not solitary and definitely one or two odd periods, but most definitely fun.

The hard part, when writing this book, was trying to work out when to stop. So, I decided to copy off the days of the week and end with Sunday. That's right, end. Now, I know the proper way is Sunday as the first day of the week. But where I grew up it was the END of the week and Monday was the beginning of the next. A new start for workers, school kids and mams.

"Bloody Monday. I've got to start doing the same bloody thing all over a soddin' gain."

There's still loads more to tell you, though. I suppose if enough of you buy this one I can always do another one. Me mam's just read this bit as I'm typing and said, "Stop being such a creep."

Thanks Mother, glad of the support.

If I ever get a book signing, I half expect her to be hanging around outside with a placard saying 'DON'T BUY THAT BOOK - SHE GAVE ME VARICOSE VEINS,' and accosting customers as they go in.

"I found out she was running errands for some lazy trollop up the road and she wouldn't even go to the downstairs shops for me. After all I've done for her."

By this point you might even hear me shouting back.

"I DIDN'T ASK TO BE BORN!"

She actually did that once. The placard thing, I mean. Stood outside Curry's in Bury. Some dispute over a microwave cooker, but I'll tell you about that next time ...

I'll also tell you about sister number two's money-making schemes, including one almost unbelievable incident (but believe you me it's true!) involving offering other kids the chance to either give her a penny or get their pants pulled down. I kid you not. Typical short kid, spiteful!

I'll also look at my years in Barbados. You can take the girl out of Collyhurst ... Relaxing in paradise and missing bonfire night. As for Christmas on the beach, well, it just can't compare to opening your window on Christmas morning and seeing the railway junction box covered in snow and nowt but pigeon footsteps on the pavement outside ... magic.

Let's not forget number three either, 'r 'manda. I still haven't covered 'let's all pretend she doesn't exist' fully and I haven't even touched on 'pretending a red hot chilli was fruit.' So there's plenty to come from her.

There'll be more on all the others and number six, 'r Tracey, will play more of a part in my adventures. I was old enough to regard her as a pretend daughter, so she mainly just did the cutest things and didn't annoy me as much as the others did. But she more than made up for it as she grew up, the little s**t.

The 'Chosen One' will be covered in a bit more detail, too. One of my favourite tales (although not at the time) is 'which one of you little sods put a dress on my son?'

More too on the Langley years, where we lived in an actual house after years in our beloved flat in Collyhurst. Luckily, we had experienced stairs at Nana's so we weren't too flummoxed at having bedrooms not next to the living room. I became a teenager there, too. Wonderful memories for me mam, I'm sure!

It wasn't all fun, either. There was tragedy, too. We lost Granddad in 1970. Manchester Arndale is a bugger to find your way round. Only joking, it wasn't built till 1975. I meant Granddad died, and you know what they say. 'It only takes one.' Once he went it seemed like we 'lost' someone every five minutes. I ate more ham butties at wakes than I did at home. But that was partly because Mam had decided to become a vegetarian. The silver lining in that cloud being ... no more stew.

The '70s also saw the emergence of 'cultural' me. All it took was one episode of *Roots* for my new responses to Mam to emerge.

"Why should I do that? I'm not a slave."

"Oh, after what your people did to my people you expect me to wash pots?"

Mam was consistent throughout, both in her devotion to being a mother and her responses to my teenage angst.

"Shut your gob and get it done, or I'll show you slavery, you cheeky cow."

So, there we go. I hope you have enjoyed, and if you are also blessed to be a Mancunian or indeed a Northerner, can relate to some of my little tales.

I won't end on goodbye. That's not Manc at all. I'll just say ta-ra for now and I'll see you later.

ABOUT THE AUTHOR

Born in 1960 to an English mother and Barbadian father, the author spent her early childhood growing up in the Manchester suburbs of Moston and Collyhurst.

After living for 3 years in Barbados as a teenager, she returned to her hometown where she has lived ever since.

A variety of jobs from sales assistant to cleaning company area manager have helped pay the bills but she has always desired to be a 'proper' writer.

She currently resides in North Manchester and is a proud Mum of three and Nana to three beautiful grandchildren.

PLATES

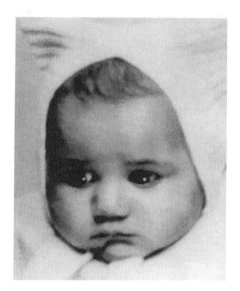

Me at 3 months. Not impressed with the cat's ears.

Mam, Dad and me (4 months old)

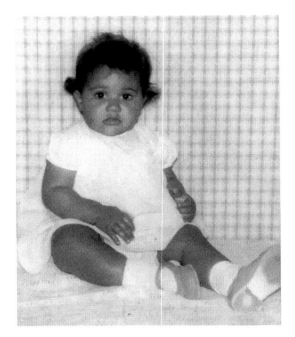

Me on my first birthday

Karin. Amanda and me aged 2, 1 and 4

Dad in his youth

Mam before she was 'Mam'

Me today

28246335R00096

Printed in Great Britain
by Amazon